Exam Success

Revision Guide for IGCSE Edexcel Poetry Anthology

Alison Goodall and Janet Oliver

The right of Alison Goodall and Janet Oliver to be identified as Authors of this work has been asserted by them in accordance with the Copyright, Designs and Patents Act 1988.

First published 2024.

© Alison Goodall and Janet Oliver

All rights reserved. No part of this publication may be reproduced, stored in a retrieval system or transmitted in any form or by any means, electronic, mechanical, photocopying, recording or otherwise, without the prior written permission of the Authors.

Restricted copying in the United Kingdom issued by the *Copyright Licensing Agency Ltd, Saffron House, 6-10 Kirby Street, London EC1N 8TS.*

Contents

Introduction — 3

PART I

If – *by Rudyard Kipling* — 6
Prayer Before Birth *by Louis MacNeice* — 8
Blessing *by Imtiaz Dharker* — 10
Search For My Tongue *by Sujata Bhatt* — 12
Half-past Two *by U A Fanthorpe* — 14
Piano *by D H Lawrence* — 16
Hide and Seek *by Vernon Scannell* — 18
Sonnet 116 *by William Shakespeare* — 20
La Belle Dame sans Merci *by John Keats* — 22
Poem at Thirty-Nine *by Alice Walker* — 24
War Photographer *by Carol Ann Duffy* — 26
The Tyger *by William Blake* — 28
My Last Duchess *by Robert Browning* — 30
Half-caste *by John Agard* — 32
Do not go gentle into that good night *by Dylan Thomas* — 34
Remember *by Christina Rossetti* — 36

PART II

Compare how the writers present the importance of memory in 'Piano' and 'Poem at Thirty-Nine'. — 40
Compare how the writers present childhood experiences in 'Half-past Two' and 'Hide and Seek'. — 44
Compare how the writers present relationships in 'Sonnet 116' and 'My Last Duchess'. — 48
Compare how the writers present ideas about death and mourning in 'Remember' and 'Do not go gentle'. — 52
Compare the ways the writers present the world in 'If –' and 'Prayer Before Birth'. — 56
Compare how the writers present strong feelings in 'Search For My Tongue' and 'Half-caste'. — 60
Compare how the writers present difficult situations in 'Blessing' and 'War Photographer'. — 64
Compare how the writers present ideas of power in 'The Tyger' and 'La Belle Dame sans Merci'. — 68

Themes Chart — 72
Glossary — 76

Introduction

The sixteen poems in the IGCSE Edexcel Anthology for English Literature are fantastic explorations of a wide array of themes and ideas. The poets transport us to a variety of places, from the dry heat of India to the wintry English lake where a knight wanders, alone and lost. The narrative voices are powerful and vivid: an unborn child, a daughter remembering her dead father, a man passionately in love. The emotional range is also incredible with adoration, fear, anger, grief and guilt being just some of the feelings powerfully presented to us.

So the poems are wonderful but many students often worry about how to revise them, and how to construct a clear, effective response to an exam question.

This guide aims to help you tackle your revision and excel in your final exam. It is carefully structured to build up your confidence and exam technique.

- Part 1 deals with each of the sixteen poems separately. For each poem, there is a strong, clear overview and a concise explanation of how form and structure are used in that poem. Then the poem is deconstructed - not in a line-by-line approach, but in a much more effective way. We explore just 5-7 key quotations per poem, digging deep into the language used and analysing the ideas and messages of the poem. We recommend that you use these notes to make your own flashcards or mind maps so that you are confident that you can write about these key quotations with the language analysis woven in.

- Part 2 takes eight exam questions and demonstrates how to plan answers for these that cover the key skills. We use a table to show how to consistently compare the ideas or themes in the poems. After each plan, there is a full model essay that would receive top marks in an exam. These essays are designed to help you hone your own essay style and understand how to cover all the skills that the examiner is looking for.

- Part 3 is the final section which allows you the opportunity to practise your own essay planning, using some question prompts and your own grids.

We hope you find this guide useful. Good luck with your exams!

PART 1

Exam Success: Revision Guide for IGCSE Edexcel Poetry Anthology

Alison Goodall and Janet Oliver

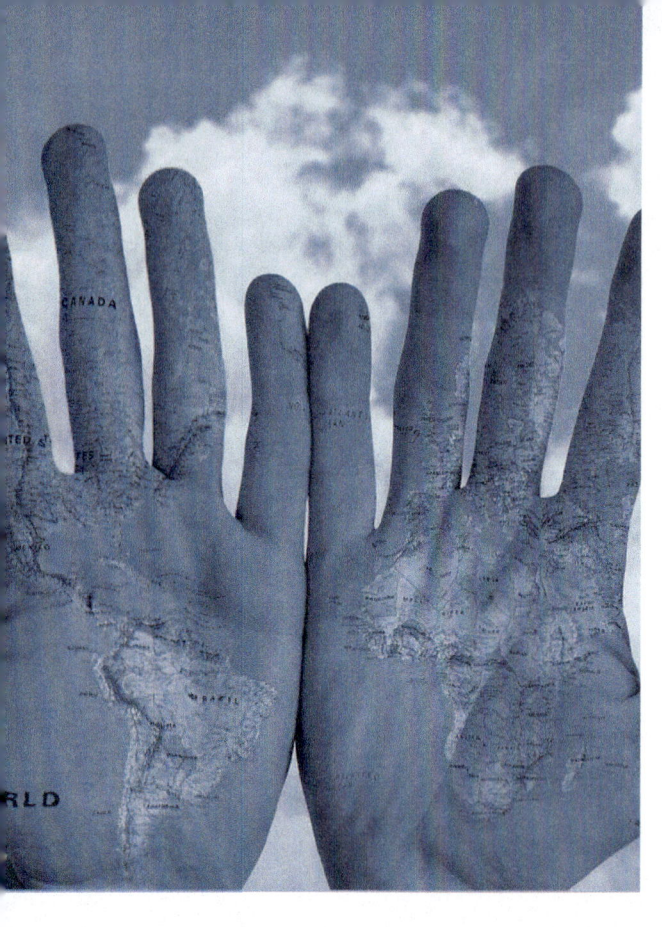

If –

by Rudyard Kipling

'If –' is a poem written by a father to his son, setting up a series of situations that the son may face with advice about how to handle these situations. The poem ends with assuring the son, and the reader, that we will have successful, moral and happy lives if we follow this advice.

Structure and Form: The whole poem is one sentence, with the poet introducing a range of hypothetical situations with the *conditional* 'if'. The final *stanza* gives us the conclusion to these situations with the word **'then'** summarising what will happen if the advice is listened to. The poet uses a regular *iambic pentameter metre* which gives the poem an energetic, inspirational tone.

'If you can keep your head when all about you/ Are losing theirs and blaming it on you'

— The poem opens with the *conditional* '**If**', and continues to use it as a *refrain*. The *conditional* offers the reader different scenarios, challenging us to consider how we would react in them.

— The opening situation suggests that the world is a turbulent, stressful place where people '**lose**' their heads and blame others. The need to be calm and logical in dangerous, volatile situations is created from the opening.

'If you can ….being lied about,/ don't deal in lies'

— There is a strong *imperative* with the word '**don't**' to reject the mendacity (trickery) of the world, a clear instruction to stay honest.

— The energy of the regular *rhythm* that weaves its way throughout the poem captures a sense of determined enthusiasm, so that the reader is convinced that it is possible to stay true and strong even in a deceitful world.

'Or watch the things you gave your life to, broken, And stoop and build 'em up with worn-out tools'

— The speaker encourages us to be resilient when life throws us challenges.

— The *verb* '**watch**' creates a sense of passive helplessness in that sometimes we have no control over what happens to us.

- The line ends with the *verb* **'broken'** and its connotations of destruction. The *plosive* **'b'** perhaps suggests a sense of bitterness at how the achievements of our lives can be wrecked.

- However, the next line begins with the *fronted conjunction* **'And'** which implies that this anger and despair can quickly be overcome.

- The *dynamic verbs* **'stoop'** and **'build'** create a sense of energetic action. We are encouraged to pick ourselves up after failure and start again, proving our resilience in the face of adversity.

- This is added to with the *word* **'wornout'** which implies that sometimes the resources we have available are limited or substandard. Despite this, we can still succeed if we are strong and determined.

'If you can fill the unforgiving minute/ With sixty seconds' worth of distance run'

- The relentless passing of time is captured in the *metaphor* of the minute being **'unforgiving'**. The speaker acknowledges that time will not stand still or be controlled by us.

- Then the next line changes the minute to **'sixty seconds' worth of distance run'**. The reduction to seconds suggests that life must be lived to the maximum, that if we put effort into our lives then we will be fulfilled.

'Yours is the Earth and everything that's in it/ And- which is more- you'll be a Man, my son!'

- The final *stanza* changes the pattern as Kipling moves to his conclusion: that if we follow his advice, then we will control our destiny on this earth and live life to the full.

- We will also be a **'Man'**, with all the connotations of strength and honour that the capitalisation implies.

- The strong *declarative sentence* shows how following the advice will lead to being successful.

- Kipling was writing to his son, giving him a personal instruction manual to deal with life but the poem's advice resonates with us all.

- The final *exclamatory statement* captures the writer's excitement that his child is becoming a man with all that this embodies.

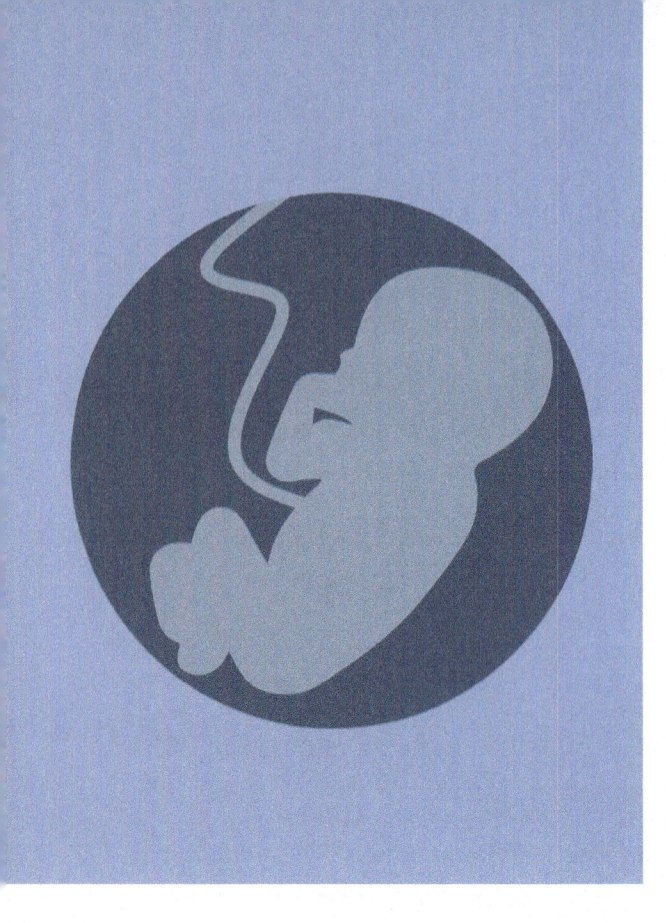

Prayer Before Birth
by Louis MacNeice

In 'Prayer Before Birth', MacNeice assumes the persona of a foetus who is praying for safety and help in the terrifying and dangerous world they are about to enter, but finding little comfort from a silent unresponsive god.

Structure and Form: The poem is a ***dramatic monologue***, with the voice of an unborn child. The structure is irregular, perhaps to reflect the chaos of the world the child is about to enter, and the ***stanzas*** become longer as the poem progresses, which could reflect the growing terror, even hysteria, of the terrified child.

'O hear me.'

- The persona prays for safety.
- The structure of the poem follows that of a prayer with the ***repeated*** structure of every ***stanza*** beginning with **'I am not yet born'** and concluding with **'me'**.
- This helps create the strong sense of the foetus and their huge worries and concerns about entering the world.

'bloodsucking bat or the rat or the stoat or the/ club-footed ghoul'.

- The child is initially scared of animals and ghosts.
- The ***polysyndetic list*** creates a childish tone and captures the persona's rising fears as they add to its fantasy list of nighttime terrors, almost with a nursery rhyme feel.
- This creates empathy for the little baby and its innocent fears.

'fear that the human race may with tall walls wall me, with strong drugs dope me, with wise lies lure me, on black racks rack me, in blood-baths roll me.'

- The persona is already aware of the slick lies and insincerity of the human race who will **'with wise lies lure me'**.

- The *alliteration* captures how slick and skilful those who deceive are, showing how easy it will be for the baby to be tricked. There is a helplessness, almost an acceptance, about how deceit and lies will prevail.

- The *list* creates a terrifying and violent portrait of inevitable suffering- and there is anger perhaps from the unborn child at the prospect of pain from the brutal human society they are about to join.

'make me a cog in a machine'

- The unborn child will give up their identity to conform. The *metaphor* **'make me a cog in a machine'** reinforces this.

- There is a reference to mechanical automation, often associated with profit. The persona knows that they will simply become one small piece in a larger mechanism. This *metaphor* perhaps refers to how industrialisation damages people as they work for material gain.

- Alternatively, it could refer to how, when we become part of society, we give up our individuality and behave like robots or machines.

'water to dandle me, grass to grow for me, trees to talk to me, sky to sing to me, birds and a white light in the back of my mind to guide me.'

- The persona asks for a connection with nature.

- There is a feeling of anticipation created through the *alliteration* and lyrical *rhythm*. There is hope that the foetus will enjoy a harmony with nature that will allow their individuality to flourish and to retain a sense of morality.

- The *metaphor* of the **'white light'**, symbol of bright hope and clarity, as a guiding force, gives us hope that the persona will use nature to resist the evil of the world and keep their inherent goodness intact.

'Let them not make me a stone and let them not spill me./ Otherwise kill me.'

- The final *stanza* marks a shift from the earlier pattern: this *stanza* is only two lines and loses the **'I am not yet born; O…'**

- This perhaps shows the speaker's vulnerability, that they have stopped asking for help as they know there is no help coming.

- The persona does not want to be a **'stone'**, something with no emotions, or to lose their identity through being **'spill'**(ed).

- The persona wants to die before birth if it means life will lead to them becoming emotionless or without personality.

- MacNeice ends his poem asking us to consider the world unborn children are entering.

Blessing
by Imtiaz Dharker

Dharker focuses on a community in India's constant struggle to survive and access fresh water. She describes the joy a burst water pipe brings to the suffering people in the slums of Mumbai.

Structure and Form: The poem is written in *free verse*. The first two *stanzas* outline the problem of the lack of water in Mumbai with short, stark *stanzas* that expose the issue. The third *stanza* relates the moment that the pipe bursts, and is much longer, with *enjambment* capturing the gushing flow of water and the hasty movements of the people to collect it. The final *stanza* ends with the children enjoying the unexpected treat of playing in the water.

'The skin cracks like a pod./ There never is enough water.'

— Dharker transports us to the vicious heat of India.

— The *simile* captures the human skin cracking in the brutal heat; the *consonantal* **'k'** sounds mimic the pain of this.

— Alternatively, the **'skin'** could refer to the surface of the land, drained of all moisture by the blazing sun.

— **'pod'** implies regeneration and growth but here, without moisture, we are reminded of how fragile life is.

— The second line is bare and matter-of-fact in *tone* as we are told clearly of the constant lack of water.

— **'never'** reminds us how this challenging situation is permanent.

'Imagine the drip'

— Dharker asks us to **'Imagine the drip'** of water. Through the *imperative verb* **'Imagine'**, she is challenging us, complacently living with the luxury of running water, to put ourselves into the lives of India's poor where the drip of water is something special.

'voice of a kindly god'

— The poet describes the dripping water as the **'voice of a kindly god'**.

- Perhaps there is an ironic **tone** here, as we wonder how kind the gods really are. The poet perhaps questions whether the gods are kind when they only send a **'drip'** of water, and do not protect the people who die daily through lack of fresh water.

'The municipal pipe bursts, silver crashes to the ground'

- **Auditory imagery** is used to capture the sound of the water pipe breaking open. The **dynamic verbs 'bursts'** and **'crashes'** work with the **enjambment** to create a sense of energetic movement as the water pumps out.
- The water is referred to as **'silver'** with the clear connotations that the water is incredibly valuable.
- Silver is also shiny, perhaps capturing the way the water catches the light.

'and the flow has found a roar of tongues'

- More **auditory imagery** is used as the **verb 'roar'** captures the excitement of the people as they call out at the unexpected, welcome event.
- Alternatively, **'roar'** is an animal sound, perhaps suggesting how the lack of water has dehumanised the people of the slums, reducing them to survival mode as they rush for the water.

'screaming in the liquid sun'

- The poem ends with more sounds as the children play in the water.
- The **phrase 'screaming in the liquid sun'** is one of pure joy and appreciation, enhanced by the **image** of light, **symbol** of warmth and hope.

'blessing sings over their small bones.'

- The **verb 'sings'** suggests the voice of the god can now be clearly heard as the children of the slum benefit from the burst water pipe.
- Yet the final **noun phrase 'small bones'** reminds us of how frail and vulnerable the children are and that the scarcity of water will return.
- The water pipe burst is only a temporary respite, and Dharker ends her poem with a reminder of the deprivation of the slums.

Search For My Tongue
by Sujata Bhatt

The poem powerfully explores ideas of language and identity as the persona tells us her fears of forgetting her original language, her mother tongue, as she lives in a foreign country.

Structure and Form: The unusual structure captures the central ideas in the poem. The first **stanza** explores her anxiety and frustrations of not using her mother tongue. The second **stanza** is in Gujarati, graphically capturing how her mother tongue is beautiful and never forgotten. The final **stanza** repeats the words of the second but this time in English, so that we can understand her hope and joy as she remembers her native language.

'Search For My Tongue'

— Even the title emphasises the importance of finding our roots. The speaker sets up the idea of our language being closely linked to our heritage.

— The *word* **'search'** shows us how she is actively looking for her identity by trying to regain the language of her childhood, her mother tongue.

— The *possessive pronoun* **'my'** creates a sense of an intense personal connection with her native language.

'You ask me' and 'I ask you'

— The poem *opens* with a sense of an on-going conversation.

— Although Bhatt is on a personal journey, we, the reader, are immediately immersed into the poem through this *direct address*.

— The *tone* is confrontational and perhaps one of frustration as she challenges us to imagine what it must be like to struggle with expressing ourselves.

'lost...the mother tongue'

— The *phrase* **'mother tongue'** implies safety, closeness and support. The person who traditionally looks after us most when we are babies is our mothers. We acquire language throughout our childhood, and this is one of the many things that defines us and stays with us.

— However, the speaker has **'lost'** this tongue which must mean she feels adrift and disconnected from her roots. There is a feeling of alienation and sadness here.

'foreign tongue'

— She calls the language of the country she lives in a **'foreign tongue'**.

— The *phrase* suggests the alien and unknown, adding onto the feelings that she doesn't belong and has a fragmented identity.

'rot,/ rot and die in your mouth'

— There is a feeling of anger or maybe sadness that she has lost something so important.

— There is also perhaps a sense of disgust at her lost language as she talks about the mother tongue with the revolting *vocabulary* **'rot,/ rot and die in your mouth.'**

— The way the verb **'rot'** ends one line and then is immediately *repeated* at the start of the next powerfully captures the extent of her anger at the disappearance of her language.

— The *consonantal* sounds **'rot' 'spit'** capture her frustration. The *monosyllabic* words are stilted; Bhatt uses simple language, reflecting her lack of connection with the language she has to use in order to communicate.

મને હતું કે આખૂખી ભ આખૂખી ભાષા

— Yet in the middle, the structure changes suddenly and dramatically with the *stanza* in Gujarati. By placing the Gujarati in the middle, she shows its central importance to her as a person.

— There is a sense of pride in the beautiful script.

— The Gujarati script also forces the reader to understand her feeling of alienation. Bhatt is educating us, ensuring that we can begin to understand the lives of immigrants who do not have English as a first language.

'grows…grows…it blossoms'

— The poem *ends* on a note of hope as she rediscovers her mother tongue.

— The *repetition* of **'grow'** creates a powerful sense of energy, enhanced by the unfolding *clauses* which build a sense of development, and the poem ends with a sense of celebration that she has regained her language and her identity.

— She uses an extended *metaphor* of a flourishing plant that **'blossoms'** and so captures ideas of hope and rejuvenation

Half-past Two
by U A Fanthorpe

In the poem, Fanthorpe explores the notion of time as seen through the eyes of a small boy who has been given detention by his teacher for some unknown misdemeanour. The boy has not yet learned to read a clock so fails to understand how long he has to stay behind in the classroom.

Structure and Form: The poem is written in *free verse*, which gives it a conversational tone as if the boy is recalling the events of his childhood. There are eleven *tercets* (*stanzas* containing three lines), which give structure to the memory. Line lengths are irregular, some only containing six *syllables*, whilst others contain as many as thirteen. These lines create the sense of time becoming elongated (stretched out) as the boy sits waiting for his detention to end.

'Once upon a schooltime'

— A young boy has misbehaved at school and his teacher has put him in detention until '**half-past two**'. Having no concept of how to read a clock, the boy enters into a mysterious world where time has no meaning.

— The poem begins by echoing the opening of a fairy tale, immediately creating a sense of a world that exists outside of the adult world that is strictly governed by time.

— The *compound word* '**schooltime**' provides a glimpse into the boy's perception of time as one that is linked to everyday activities, continued later in the poem with '**Gettinguptime**' and '**timeyouwereofftime**'.

'And She said he'd done Something Very Wrong'

— The use of the *pronouns* '**he**' / '**She**' and the anonymity it creates adds to the sense of a universal experience: this could be the story of any child in any classroom. As the misdemeanour is ambiguous (unclear), the reader can relate the authoritarian voice of the teacher to their own experiences of childhood punishments.

— The *capitalisation* of the *adverb*, '**Very**' and the *adjective*, '**Wrong**' indicates the angry tone of the teacher and emphasises the words imprinted on the boy's memory. Indeed, the teacher was so angry with the boy that she forgot that he did not know how to tell the time, and the boy is so intimidated by the admonishment (telling off) that he dare not ask.

'He knew the clockface, the little eyes/ And two long legs for walking'

— Although the boy knew that time was linked to certain events like getting up, going to school and even kissing grandma, he had no understanding of the function of a clock.

— The *personification* of the clock's features highlight the boy's childlike perception of time as he imagines the hour and minute hands **'walking'** around the face which looks over him with **'little eyes'**.

— The *transitive verb* **'knew'** shows that the boy is familiar with the physical object that he would see every day in the classroom; however, he has no concept of time itself.

— *Alliteration* and *assonance* in **'long legs for walking'** are used to create a feeling of time extending, as it must have felt to the young boy in the schoolroom.

'he'd escaped for ever … Into the smell of old chrysanthemums …silent noise …the air outside the window, into ever'

— Previously, time has been measured in small actions and events, but now the boy is faced with a seemingly endless period of waiting. He becomes absorbed by the sights, sounds and smells of the classroom.

— *Anaphora* is used in the repetition of **'into the …'** and this draws the reader into this world as we fall mysteriously under the spell of the past.

— The *vivid sensory description* of the classroom as experienced by the boy brings the reader into the timeless world he has entered as he has no idea when, or if, his normal life will ever resume. The flowers are **'old'** and the sound of his hangnail is **'silent'**. These *adjectives* serve to recreate a strange, almost otherworldly atmosphere where time is suspended.

— The *verb* **'escaped'** together with the *intensifier* **'for ever'** create a sense of freedom and liberation from the strict authoritarian order of the school day. The world he now occupies is surreal and otherworldly, drawing our attention back to the hint of fairy tale established in the first line of the poem.

'time hides tick-less waiting to be born.'

— At the end of the poem, the teacher remembers the boy in detention and releases him from the timeless confines of the classroom; however, the memory of the incident stays with him.

— Time is *personified* as we are shown the profound effect this experience had on the boy as an adult. He has **'never forgot'** how he entered a world where time did not exist, held in a state before the clock began to rule our lives.

— The *onomatopoeia* created in **'time'** and **'tick-less'** echoes the ticking of a clock, which had been stalled for the duration of the detention.

Piano

by D H Lawrence

'Piano' is a poem which explores the power of childhood memories and how an event in the present can transport one back to reflect nostalgically on the past. Memories of childhood bring both joy and longing for a world to which we can never return.

Structure and Form: The poem consists of three **quatrains** (four lines in each **stanza**), composed of two **rhyming couplets**. The variety of line lengths and rhythms create a reflective tone and echo the music as it ebbs and flows in his memory. This is heightened by the use of the **rhyming couplets** that provide a clear structure and a sense of predictability, which is somehow comforting.

'Softly, in the dusk, a woman is singing to me;'

— The poem begins with the speaker listening to a woman singing. The sound transports him back to a childhood memory of his mother playing the piano.

— The **adverbial phrase** in the first line of the poem creates a warm and intimate feeling: the use of **sibilance** giving the line a soft and seductive tone.

— The setting is dusk, a magical time when the distinction between day and night becomes blurred and obscure. **Symbolically,** this alludes to the blurring of past and present, adulthood and childhood that the speaker is about to experience.

— Ending the line with the **personal pronoun 'me'** focuses the attention on the speaker in this **first-person narrative**. It suggests the power that music has to create a unique and highly personal experience.

'in the boom of the tingling strings'

— The childhood world that is created is one where the speaker is literally and metaphorically immersed in music. The **preposition 'in'** implies that the boy is a part of the instrument itself.

— **Sensory language** including the **onomatopoeic 'boom'** recreates a world where music had such a profound and long-lasting effect on him, the **'tingling strings'** an extension of his own heightened emotions. As well as an auditory description, the **noun 'boom'** is reminiscent of 'womb' creating a nurturing and protective environment.

'the insidious mastery of song/ Betrays me back,'

— The speaker is unwillingly pulled back into the past - the memory is warm and intimate but the longing he feels for a return to this state is unbearable. Music is seen as having the power to evoke strong emotions and memories without the listener's consent. The *adjective* **'insidious'** portrays music as cunning and sly: something that creeps up on you before you are aware of its presence.

— The *personification* of music as something that **'betrays'** the speaker, furthers the idea that music is somehow treacherous and deceitful: the speaker is tricked into returning to his childhood memory.

— *Sibilance* is used to create a sinister and menacing tone, whilst the *alliterative* **'betrays…back'** adds a forceful note to the power of music.

'till the heart of me weeps to belong/ To the old Sunday evenings at home'

— The *personification* of the speaker's heart, *symbolically* portrayed as the centre of our emotions, emphasises his desperate yearning for the warmth and comfort of childhood. The description of **'home'** is nostalgic and filled with a deep sense of longing.

— The use of *enjambment* creates a link between the present and the past as the speaker mourns the loss of childhood. Even though music can transport him back temporarily to the warmth of his childhood home, it comes with the understanding that he must always return to the present.

— The *present continuous tense* evident in **'weeps to belong'** conveys the enduring emotional pull to his past. Using the *verb* **'belong'** to end the line highlights the intense desire of the speaker to stay in the idyllic childhood world that is evoked by the music. He feels connected to the past but at the same time forever distanced, emphasised by the *adjective* **'old'**.

'my manhood is cast/ Down in the flood of remembrance'

— Back in the present, the singer performs **'in vain'**. The lure of the past is too strong and the music of the present becomes a **'clamour'** rather than the softness described in the first stanza.

— The *personal possessive pronoun* **'my'** keeps his reaction very much in the individual experience of the speaker as the singer has transported him back to a time of warmth, affection and comfort. Everything that he has become as an adult – his **'manhood'**- is lost in the waves of emotion that overwhelm him.

— The speaker seems powerless to prevent his memories from impacting his adult self. Any protective shield of masculinity is broken down and overcome by the **'flood'** of his childhood recollections.

'I weep like a child for the past.'

— At the end of the poem, the speaker is left emotionally drained as his adult rationality is stripped away in favour of the raw reaction of a child. The *simile* exposes the power that music can have on the listener: it can be both uplifting and destructive.

Hide and Seek
by Vernon Scannell

Scannell uses a second-person narrative voice to give advice on how to win a game of hide-and-seek. The poem is an ***extended metaphor***, highlighting the dangers of socially isolating oneself and how life's seeming victories can lead to disappointment and loneliness.

Structure and Form: The poem is written as a ***stream of consciousness*** in ***free verse***. The twenty-seven lines, which are undivided by any ***stanza*** breaks, incorporate ***direct speech*** and a series of ***imperatives*** to create an excitable and nervous tension, echoing the feelings of the child hiding in the shed. Interspersed within the structure of the poem, several ***rhyming couplets*** create a cohesive effect, linking the future consequences to the actions of the child.

'Call out. Call loud: 'I'm ready! Come and find me!'

— The poem begins at the start of the game as the child has hidden in a garden shed and is drawing the seekers' attention to the fact that he is ready to be sought. The series of short ***imperative sentences*** create a clear and confident voice. The child considers himself an expert in the game and the instruction to **'Call loud'** conveys a sense that the child has no concern at being caught. He is excited for the game to begin. The ***tone*** is instructive and overly-confident.

— ***Exclamatory sentences*** **'I'm ready! Come and find me!'** create an air of excitement and anticipation as if the child is taunting the seekers, safe in the knowledge that he will not be caught.

— But who is the **'you'** that the speaker is addressing? The voice could be an ***internal monologue***, a guide created by the child and acting as a fellow conspirator in this game of hide and seek. Or the speaker could be addressing **'you'** the reader, giving clear instructions on how to play and win the game. Whether the speaker is addressing himself or the reader, the outcome is the same. The game ends with disappointment and loss.

'The sacks… smell like the seaside… salty dark… the dark damp smell of sand'

— The recurring ***image*** of the sea and in particular the sandbags behind which the boy is hiding, initially conveys a feeling of protection and familiarity. The seaside has positive connotations, of wide expanses of sand, salty sea air and childhood holidays. The boy immerses himself in the image of this environment to deflect his thoughts from the darkness of the shed.

— Scannell uses ***synaesthesia*** to blend the literal and the metaphorical worlds together as the hider sits in the '**salty dark**'.

— As time goes on and the boy is still undiscovered, his environment becomes cold and uncomfortable. The *pre-modifiers* '**dark damp**' convey a more oppressive and claustrophobic atmosphere to his hiding place as the feelings of loneliness and isolation replace his initial excitement.

'Don't breathe. Don't move. Stay dumb. Hide in your blindness'

— As the boy waits apprehensively in his hiding place, he hears the voices of the seekers coming closer. The series of *imperative verbs* emphasised by the *anaphora* used at the start of the line create drama and tension as the words act as a warning against the approaching danger.

— *Monosyllabic words* and repetitive use of *caesura* add to the staccato *rhythm* of the line, representative of the boy's thumping heartbeat.

— The hider in the shed is told to '**Stay dumb**'. Literally, the command is referring to his need for silence but *metaphorically*, the speaker could be commenting on the act of socially isolating oneself as foolish.

— The emphasis placed on the *abstract noun* '**blindness**' as the only *polysyllabic word* in the line, develops the idea that to hide away from society, or become isolated by placing yourself in a superior position to others, is restrictive and counter-productive. The boy cannot see what is happening.

'someone stumbles, mutters;/ Their words and laughter scuffle'

— In contrast to the *restrictive verbs* '**Stay…Hide**', in the previous line, the *active verbs* '**stumbles, mutters…scuffle**' bring a child-like excitement to the poem. The movements are clumsy and awkward as the children grope around in the darkness of the shed.

— As the seekers delight in the game, bonded together by their shared experience, the lone hider listens to their childish giggles. *Personification* is used to suggest the way that the children's voices trip over one another in muffled cries of youthful exuberance.

'Yes, here you are. But where are they who sought you?'

— The *declarative sentence* which opens the final line reinforces the confident and assured voice of the speaker and announces the victory which he assumes is his. The *interjection* '**Yes**' gives the line a triumphant sound, reflecting the feeling of superiority felt by the hider. But it is a Pyrrhic victory (a victory that comes at a great cost and, therefore, worthless): the boy may have won the game but in doing so, he has lost himself.

— The poem ends with a *rhetorical question*, which adds a tentative, uncertain *tone* to the otherwise confident voice of the speaker. Whilst the hider has been feeling smug and secure in his victory, the seekers have lost interest and gone home.

Revision Guide for IGCSE Edexcel Poetry Anthology | 19

Sonnet 116
by William Shakespeare

In 'Sonnet 116', Shakespeare describes the enduring nature of true love as something which is fixed and unwavering, unchanged by time or circumstances.

Structure and Form: 'Sonnet 116' is a traditional Shakespearean *sonnet* consisting of fourteen lines divided into three *quatrains* and a *rhyming couplet*. The first twelve lines introduce a theme or conflict, which is then resolved or concluded in the second half of the poem. This change in the content of the poem is called the *volta*. Shakespeare's use of *iambic pentameter* throughout the poem, reflects the unwavering nature of his love.

'Let me not to the marriage of true minds/ Admit impediments;'

— The opening lines are reminiscent of the wedding vows of Elizabethan England when the bride and groom were asked if they knew of any **'impediments'** (or obstacles) to the marriage.

— The speaker declares that nothing should stand in the way of two people who are truly in love. The *verb* **'admit'** implies that true love will never allow anything to change its course.

— The union that is described is one of **'true minds'**. The *pre-modifier* **'true'** could suggest a marriage based on an equal understanding of love: a permanent and enduring state which does not alter as the relationship progresses.

'O no, it is an ever-fixed mark/ That looks on tempests and is never shaken;'

— The *declamatory* at the start of line 5 signifies a movement in the argument from a general assertion of love being an unchanging state, to specific examples of love's qualities.

— In the Elizabethan era, mariners would depend on the North Star, the **'ever-fixed mark'**, to navigate their way across the ocean.

— The *metaphor* confirms the speaker's view of love. By comparing love to a star, which guides sailors as they navigate rough seas, he suggests that love is a constant point of reference and something that can be trusted, even if all around you is turmoil.

— *Iambic pentameter* is used to provide a smooth and fluent rhythm, reflecting the way that love can guide you smoothly through life's difficulties.

'Love's not Time's fool, though rosy lips and cheeks/ Within his bending sickle's compass come;'

— In the third *quatrain*, the speaker returns to the idea of love as an enduring and unwavering state of being. Time is *personified* as an adversary who destroys the vitality and youthfulness of a loved one as indicated by the *adjective* 'rosy' when describing their physical features.

— Time is also depicted with a 'sickle', the favoured instrument of Death: in this instance Time is seen as wielding a weapon to break the bond between the lovers. The harsh *alliteration* evidenced in 'si**ck**le's **c**ompass **c**ome' highlights the cruelty of Time as it ravages youth's beauty.

— Love is also *personified* as it is not '**Time's fool**'. The *possessive noun* suggests that Time tries to make an idiot of Love by ruining the physical appearance of the loved one and thus destroying the concept of enduring love.

— However, the speaker suggests that Love is not deceived by Time. Love does not change even if beauty is destroyed because love is of '**true minds**' and does not depend on physical attributes.

'Love alters not with his brief hours and weeks, But bears it out even to the edge of doom.'

— The speaker insists on true love as being unstoppable even to the point of death. The *metaphor* '**edge of doom**' highlights the moment that the lovers must separate and is reminiscent of the marriage vows (also alluded to in the opening lines of the poem): 'till death us do part'.

— The *abstract noun* '**doom**' represents a catastrophic time when all life ends. To the speaker to be parted from his loved one suggests not only the end of his life but the end of all life.

— The *end-stopped* line adds a definitive tone to the argument and a finality to the relationship. Death is the only impediment that Love cannot overcome.

'If this be error and upon me prov'd, I never writ, nor no man ever lov'd.'

— The poem ends with a *rhyming couplet*, following the traditional form of a *Shakespearean sonnet*. This shift in the abab *rhyme scheme* also indicates a shift in the ideas.

— Line 13 marks the *volta* of the *sonnet*. Here the speaker provides an emphatic conclusion to his notion of love.

— The *subordinating conjunction*, '**If**' is used to introduce the *conditional clause*, but the speaker is not providing a counter-argument. Rather, he is summarising his impassioned declaration: if he is wrong about love, then he states that he never wrote anything and no man was ever in love.

— In other words, he is certain of his argument.

La Belle Dame sans Merci
by John Keats

'La Belle Dame sans Merci' is a ballad that tells the story of a knight who falls in love with a beautiful cruel woman. This woman, who possesses magical powers, bewitches him and leaves him broken and miserable.

Structure and Form: a ***ballad*** is a poem that tells a story, usually a tragic one, and this poem certainly tells a story of suffering. The narrative is split between an unknown speaker who asks the lonely knight for his story, and the knight himself. A ***ballad*** follows a ***regular rhythm*** to maintain the momentum of the story; in this poem, the first three lines are ***iambic tetramete***r but the final line of each ***stanza*** is only five ***syllables***, and the final word is ***unstressed***. This creates a flat, defeated ***tone***, echoing the way the knight has been defeated by the woman.

'Alone and palely loitering'

— The poem opens with a speaker asking a question of a knight who is '**alone and palely loitering**'.

— The knight is immediately established as isolated and abandoned. The ***phrase*** '**palely loitering**' suggests that he has lost his natural healthy colour, and is perhaps ill.

— There is a lack of purpose in the ***verb*** '**loitering**' which reveals how the witch has stripped him of motivation and action. Traditionally, Mediaeval knights are dynamic heroes in control of their own adventures and destinies yet in the poem the knight is a helpless victim, reflecting how Keats is subverting the expectations of the reader.

— The question is ***repeated*** as a ***hook*** as we wonder, along with the speaker, what has happened to the knight to leave him in such a state.

'Full beautiful - a faery's child,... And her eyes were wild.'

— In ***stanza*** 4, the knight takes over the narrative and tells his story of how he met a woman who is '**full beautiful - a faery's child…and her eyes were wild.**'

— The woman is positioned as desirable- the ***intensifier*** '**full**' works with the ***adjective*** '**beautiful**' to create an impression of a stunning woman. Certainly, in the male speaker's view, she is defined first by her physical attraction.

— She is unusual as she is a '**faery's child**' and while this perhaps adds to her attraction in the eyes of the knight, it also establishes her as possibly dangerous, operating under different rules to

- conventional society.
  - This idea is added to with the description of her **'wild'** eyes, suggesting a savage side, unconstrained by civilised ways to behave.
  - The *rhyme scheme* is consistent throughout the poem which fits in with the genre of a **ballad**. Here, the *rhyme* links the words **'faery's child'** with **'wild'** which in turn highlight the supernatural element to the story and the savage power of the fierce belle dame who is the daughter of a magical being.

'I made a garland for her head…. I set her on my pacing steed,'

- The knight immediately falls under the woman's spell.
- The *simple sentences* capture his desire to please his new love. Interestingly, both actions emasculate the knight. He surrenders his male power by placing the woman on his horse; traditionally, a knight is placed high above others on his fast powerful horse, yet here the woman is elevated, perhaps showing the way she has taken control.
- Similarly, the knight undertakes the domestic feminine task of weaving flowers to decorate the woman's head, again showing how she has undermined his masculine authority.

'pale kings, and princes too/ Pale warriors, death-pale …They cried - 'La Belle Dame sans Merci/ Thee hath in thrall!''

- The knight dreams of the other men who have been bewitched by the belle dame.
- The *repetition* of **'pale'** reminds us of the knight's description at the start. All these powerful men of wealth and status are drained of their vitality- no one is safe from the woman's spells and charms. The voices of the men who **'cried'** adds to the sense of drama as we hear their urgent calls of warning.

'And no birds sing.'

- The poem ends with the knight echoing the original speaker's words that **'no birds sing'**.
- Now the reader understands why the knight is alone and without purpose, and understands his despair. The *pathetic fallacy* of the dead winter landscape and the absence of life and sound from the birds, powerfully capture the bleak ending and the knight's hopelessness.
- The *cyclical structure* echoes the hopeless state that the knight is trapped within, and suggests that other men will fall victim to the beautiful **'faery's child'**.

Poem at Thirty-Nine
by Alice Walker

In this poem, Walker shares memories of her father who has passed away. She thinks he would be proud of the person she has become.

Structure and Form: The poem is written in *free verse* using *irregular line lengths* and a loose structure to represent how memories drift in and out of the writer's mind. The overall effect is a *stream of consciousness* that allows us to see snippets of her father's life. The lack of a consistent *rhythm* and *rhyme scheme* adds to the effect of memories that arrive in an unpredictable and unrestrained way.

'How I miss my father.'

— The opening line indicates that Walker's father has passed away and that this is a *eulogy* written by the poet to reminisce about his life. Using the *first person* **'I'** and the *possessive pronoun* **'my'** shows that this is an intensely personal poem.

— The *declarative sentence* that is repeated on line 25 creates a nostalgic *tone*. Here the line is *end-stopped*, which adds to the strength of feeling.

— Using *enjambment* in lines 2 – 5 provides a contrast to the *end-stopped* first line and heightens the effect of this initial sentiment. It also establishes the style of the poem as a *stream of consciousness*.

'I learned to see/ bits of paper as a way/ to escape the life he knew…'

— There is a sense that the poet's father went through financial hardship when she was growing up.

— Literally, paper money leads to a more financially stable life without the difficulties her father faced, which the poet remembers regretfully as making him **'tired'**. **Metaphorically**, the **'bits of paper'** could relate to Walker's own writing which has resulted in her success in life as a famous author and poet.

— The *varied line lengths* together with the use of *enjambment* highlight the way in which Walker's memories are fragmentary. Ideas merge into one another as the impact of her father's lessons show his significance on her life and career.

- The *verb* **'escape'** suggests liberation from the entrapment of poverty and demonstrates how Walker was able to leave behind the austerity of her childhood.

'He cooked like a person/ dancing/ in a yoga meditation…'

- The use of food and cooking as a *motif* symbolising generosity and warmth begins on line 26. Here the *simile* conveys her appreciation of her father's vitality and energy as well as his ability to stay grounded.

- The *antithesis* of **'dancing'** and **'meditation'** highlights the unique qualities of her father: he was capable of both joyful exuberance as well as reflection and spirituality. Alternatively, the image could convey his refusal to conform: whilst others were quiet and subdued, he was **'dancing'**.

'tossing this and that/ into the pot;/ seasoning none of my life/ the same way twice;'

- The *metaphor* of cooking is extended here to incorporate the poet's way of life. She acknowledges a carefree and ad hoc approach to life using the *verb* **'tossing'** to suggest the way in which she not only throws ingredients together when she cooks, but also how her life is a combination of different elements that are never repeated.

- **'seasoning'** is used to enhance and boost the flavour of food. By using the *verb* to describe how she approaches life, Walker is suggesting that she has emulated her father's joy of creating new flavours as well as enjoying new experiences both culinary and in life itself.

- As the *metaphor* extends to feeding **'whoever strays my way'**, the *motif* of cooking is linked to generosity of spirit and a willingness to share what she has with others.

'He would have grown/ to admire … cooking, writing, chopping wood/ staring into the fire.'

- The final *stanza* of the poem focuses on the woman the poet has become, and how she thinks her father would have respected the qualities that she has developed.

- An *asyndetic list* is used to suggest the confidence and surety that the poet has in her abilities. It also implies that this list is not exhaustive and that she is proud of her independence.

- The items in the list all signify something she has learnt from her father: the **'cooking'** represents warmth and generosity; **'writing'** has resulted in financial independence; **'chopping wood'** shows her self-sufficiency; and the final act of **'staring into the fire'** implies a reflective and contemplative soul, mirroring the balance that her father demonstrated through his life.

- There is a more negative *tone* in the *phrase* **'He would have grown to admire…'** which links back to lines 22 - 23: **'my truths must have grieved him'**. The *verb phrase* **'would have grown'** suggests that, at some point, there was a conflict of opinion between father and daughter.

War Photographer
by Carol Ann Duffy

In this poem, Duffy, who was inspired by her friendship with a war photographer, explores the difficulties of a profession which means that the photographer has to record dreadful sights and experiences without being able to help.

Structure and Form: The poem follows a regular pattern of four six-line **stanzas** and a consistent **rhyme scheme** ABBCDD. This strict, unchanging pattern perhaps reflects the photographer's stoic determination to complete his job professionally in the midst of terrible chaos and suffering. The poem opens with the photographer in the process of developing photographs, and ends with the photographer coming full circle. He is flying out to another trouble spot to take more photographs which will be developed and published- and nothing will change. The *cyclical nature* of the poem illustrates how suffering will continue and shows a pessimistic view of human nature and its inability to avoid conflict.

'priest'... 'mass'

— The *religious imagery* connects the photographer to the idea of a vocational calling. Just as a priest is called by God to do God's work, it is the photographer's duty to share his images with the public in order to record the suffering.

— By using *religious imagery,* Duffy is exploring the photographer's job and his emotions surrounding it. It could be that the photographer feels overwhelming guilt for recording the suffering rather than stopping it, and is now seeking atonement (forgiveness) for this sin. Alternatively, perhaps the *religious imagery* shows the utmost respect with which the photographer handles the images of suffering.

'spools of suffering'

— The rolls of film are described as **'spools of suffering'**.

— The *sibilance* and *assonance* of the long drawn out vowel sounds capture the sense of the continuing, extended sorrow and pain of the affected people.

— A spool winds and unwinds, so the spool could be a *symbol* of the never-ending misery of people caught up in conflict.

'Solutions slop in trays'

— The photographer uses fluid in trays to develop the photographs.

- The *alliteration* illustrates the unsteady process of developing these photos. The photographer needed to be detached and professional while taking the photographs but now, in the safety of the dark room, his emotion in response to the horror is evident in his unsteady hands.

- Alternatively, it suggests the inadequacy of politics in that '**solutions**' to the world's troublespots are messy and ineffective. There is a *tone* of contempt in the use of the *verb* '**slop**' so Duffy could be expressing her low opinion of world leaders' weak and careless attempts to stop the suffering of ordinary people.

'Something is happening.'

- There is a sense of drama that marks a change in this *stanza*.

- The reader watches the photograph developing with the photographer, creating a sense of immediacy and involvement, especially as it's in the *present tense*.

'twist'

- An image on the developing photo is of a person who '**twist**(s)' into view. This could be a description of the photo as it comes into focus.

- '**twist**' is a painful *verb*, suggesting a body writhing in pain. The reader understands that this photo is of someone who is suffering, perhaps being tortured or being killed.

'prick with tears'

- The readers who see the photos in the poem are portrayed as shallow as their eyes '**prick with tears**'.

- '**prick**' suggests a tiny amount of response from the reader and shows the lack of involvement from the average Sunday paper reader, and how little they are affected by what they see and read.

- Again, Duffy challenges us and our own response to the evil taking place in the world and how we ignore it.

'he stares impassively'

- The photographer is flying off to yet another war zone.

- The *adverb* '**impassively**' shows how his emotions are now under control.

- It is as if he is resigned to the fact that his photographs make no difference yet he continues to fulfil his duty of recording.

- There is a sense of distance, of isolation, of the photographer from the general public.

The Tyger
by William Blake

'The Tyger' is a poem which uses the fictional creation of a beautiful but deadly tiger in a divine blacksmith's forge to question how and why God introduces danger and evil into the world.

Structure and Form: The poem is written in six regular **quatrains** (four-line **stanzas**) that follow a rigid **rhyme scheme** and insistent **trochaic tetrameter rhythm**. This creates a sense of the hammer relentlessly pounding in the blacksmith's forge as the tiger's shape is formed. The poem is formed from a series of increasingly challenging questions which seek to understand why God deliberately allows evil to exist in the world.

'Tyger, Tyger, burning bright'

— The poem immediately addresses the tiger, calling it '**burning bright**'.

— The **plosive alliteration** of the '**b**' sounds ensures an energetic, explosive start.

— '**burning**' suggests the deadly nature of the tiger as fire can easily become uncontrollable and destructive.

— Yet the tiger is also '**bright**' suggesting that it is glowing and beautiful.

— Blake sets up one of his many unanswered questions here as he wonders how something stunning can also be so terrible.

'What immortal hand or eye, Could frame thy fearful symmetry?'

— Blake asks a series of questions throughout the poem, asking why God would create something so lethal, and so unleash danger into the world.

— The '**immortal hand or eye**' refers to God, all-powerful and everlasting, who deliberately '**frame(s)**' or shapes the body of the tiger.

— '**fearful symmetry**' refers to the gorgeous markings of the tiger's coat. Again, the sense of the tiger's danger and beauty is evident; the **phrase** captures the perfect camouflage of the markings that allow the tiger to become a skilled hunter.

'And what shoulder, & what art,
Could twist the sinews of thy heart?'

- Here, the poet imagines the tiger being created in a blacksmith's forge with '**anvil**' and '**furnace**'.

- Blake depicts God as a strong blacksmith who can '**twist the sinews**' of the tiger's heart into place. Blake makes it clear that the existence of the tiger is no accident: it was a deliberate act of creation.

'What the hammer? what the chain…?'

- The flurry of *questions* becomes ever more insistent, as the poet's desire for answers becomes stronger.

- The *rhythm* used is *trochaic tetrameter* which reflects the pounding of the hammer in the forge, vividly conveying to the readers the enormous strength of God as he works on his creation. Alternatively, the insistent *rhythm* could capture the deliberate padding of a tiger's feet as it moves through its territory.

'Did he smile his work to see?
'Did he who made the Lamb make thee?'

- Here, the poet questions God's intentions. He asks if God was happy with his creation, whether he '**smile(d)**' at his finished product.

- The next question ponders how the same God who made the vulnerable gentle lamb can also have made the dangerous tiger- how and why God chose to put predators into the world. The *tone* is incredulous, as if the poet is struggling to understand, and seems to question God's decisions.

'What immortal hand or eye,
Dare frame thy fearful symmetry?'

- The poem ends with an almost identical *stanza* to the beginning.

- The constant questions are never answered. Blake is unable to answer the questions he poses - just as we are unable to make sense of a world where good and evil coexist.

My Last Duchess
by Robert Browning

Browning presents us with a sixteenth-century Italian Duke who is in the process of negotiating a new marriage through meeting with an envoy (messenger) from the prospective bride's father. As the Duke shows the envoy his wealth and possessions, he stops to show him a portrait of his late, dead wife. The Duke's own words imply that he ordered his wife's murder, and so Browning allows us into the mind of a cold-hearted, arrogant man whose love of power and control leads him to commit terrible acts.

Structure and Form: The poem takes the form of a *dramatic monologue* which allows us to only hear the Duke's voice and views. All others are excluded as the Duke tries to shape the envoy's view and our view of himself. His control is also seen in the structure of these lines: the *enjambment* of the poem and the continuous unbroken *stanza* shows how he controls the flow of lines.

'My Last Duchess'

— Even in the title of the poem, the Duke is presented as a man who likes to control. The *possessive pronoun* '**my**' shows that his wife belongs to him; he sees her as a possession.

— He defines her as '**last Duchess**' which implies she is one in a long list of wives, unimportant in herself.

'none puts by/ The curtain I have drawn for you, but I'

— The Duke chooses when the curtain that covers the portrait is open or closed.

— This line reflects his iron control over his wife as, even in death, he decides who will look at her. There is a huge sense of authoritarian power in the *word* '**none**' which shows how this control extends to cover everybody in his household.

— His control is also seen in the structure of these lines: the *enjambment* here captures how he controls the flow of lines.

— The *syntactical placement* of '**but I**' at the end of the line emphasises it is he who has the final command.

'my gift of a nine-hundred-years-old name'

— The Duke puts huge value on his social status as an aristocrat, a titled nobleman who has been born into a family of wealth and influence.

— The use of the ***noun*** **'gift'** captures how he chooses to share this status as he has the power to bestow (give) his high-class name on his wife. There is a sense of patronage and condescension in this phrase as there is a sense that the Duke thinks that his wife should be flattered and grateful for the **'gift'**. He is annoyed that she does not value or appreciate it.

— The ***tone*** is of arrogant pride in the fact he can trace his ancestry back so far- his family has held power for almost a millennia. There is a sense of entitlement and privilege in the phrase **'nine-hundred-years-old name'**.

'the dropping of the daylight' 'white mule' 'cherries'

— The Duchess does not share this love of status; she places her value on natural pleasures: watching the sunset, **'the dropping of the daylight'**, riding her **'white mule'**, eating **'cherries'**.

— The ***list*** here emphasises the range of these simple pleasures that are available to all people.

— It ***contrasts*** with the Duke's pleasure in his status and material goods; for example, the portrait painted by a famous artist and the bronze statue of Neptune.

'her looks went everywhere.'

— The Duke clearly disapproves of his wife's actions.

— There is a suggestion that she wasn't aloof (superior) enough, and also that she was flirtatious/unfaithful.

'I gave commands;/ Then all smiles stopped together.'

— His disapproval of her leads to him ordering his wife to be killed.

— The authoritative ***tone*** of **'I gave commands'** is highlighted by the pause at the end of the line and emphasises what comes after: the vile consequences of these commands, his wife's murder.

— The sly ***sibilance*** **'smiles stopped'** highlights the sinister nature of the killing of the Duchess.

— It is interesting that the Duke says **'all smiles stopped'**. The ***determiner*** **'all'** could perhaps suggest that his own smiles stopped as well. It is possible that he did have feelings for her after all, and that his desire for power over his wife made him go too far - a decision that he then regrets.

Revision Guide for IGCSE Edexcel Poetry Anthology | 31

Half-caste
by John Agard

'Half-caste' is a powerful poem that challenges stereotypes and discrimination through the speaker's exploration of the word 'half-caste'. This is a derogatory word for people of mixed-race, and throughout the poem, the speaker ridicules it so that the reader is encouraged to confront their own prejudices.

Structure and Form: The poem is in *free verse* with short lines and limited punctuation which creates a fast-paced poem that hammers home his message: that prejudice is wrong. The use of *phonetic spelling* and the Caribbean dialect called *Creole* work together to highlight how Agard takes control of his identity through his language.

'Half-caste'

— The title **'Half-caste'** shows how the speaker knows that he is defined by his colour. He is acknowledging how society gives him a label that is linked to his racial background.

'Excuse me
standing on one leg
I'm half-caste'

— The poem opens with a meek, humble request for the reader, or the person being addressed, to **'Excuse me'**.

— There is humour as he highlights the nonsense of the term **'half-caste'**, which implies a mixed-race person is lesser in some way- so much so that they have to stand on **'one leg'**.

'Explain yuself'

— The humorous *tone* of the humble opening *stanza* abruptly changes to a confrontational *tone* as the speaker demands that society needs to **'explain yuself'**.

— The phrase is *repeated*, putting continuous pressure on the reader to explain why we use the racist definition of people of mixed-race.

32 | *Exam Success*

'Yu mean when picasso
mix red an green
is a half-caste canvas/'

— Agard uses *imagery* to present his message that his mixed identity is beautiful by referencing art, which blends colours to create something beautiful and of high-value.

— We should extend this to race, with the message that mixed-race people should also be valued.

— He is proud of his heritage, and this is further emphasised by the lack of a capital letter for **'picasso'**. This, and the disregard throughout the poem of traditional rules of punctuation and capitalisation, captures his pride in his own language and identity.

'Ah rass'

— There is anger in the expletive **'ah rass'** which captures his disgust at the racism.

— This *phrase* forms one distinct line, suggesting how his anger spills out mid-way through his argument.

'I half-caste human being
cast half-a-shadow'

— Agard feels as if he is separated from mainstream society by being labelled **'half-caste'**.

— The line suggests that he believes that people see him as not fully human, that he is not really seen or important in society.

— This idea of a half-shadow links to Gothic ideas of the supernatural, reflecting how society often fears anyone who is different.

'but yu must come back tomorrow
wid ... de whole of yu mind'

— Agard ends his poem on a challenge., telling the reader to be more open-minded and to reject racial discrimination, to open our minds.

'an I will tell yu
de other half
of my story'

— At the very end, Agard promises that he will share his experiences and culture with us.

— There is a sense of hope that, with the end of pointless labels and discrimination, we can have a fuller, richer society.

Do not go gentle into that good night
by Dylan Thomas

'Do not go gentle into that good night' explores the ideas and feelings associated with death as Thomas urges his father, and, perhaps, the reader, to resist death and hold onto life.

Structure and Form: The poem takes the form of a *villanelle*, a nineteen-line poem that follows a *regular rhyme scheme*: ABA ABA ABA ABA ABA ABA ABAA. This strict form, combined with the ten syllable *rhythm* and regular three-line *stanzas*, suggests that Thomas is using this rigid pattern to perhaps contain his grief at the prospect of his father's approaching death. The change in pattern in the last *stanza* reflects the shift from Thomas giving advice generally to all old people to the personal, as he directly addresses his father.

'Do not go gentle into that good night'

— The speaker in Thomas' poem uses the *imperative form* in his opening line '**Do not go gentle into that good night**'.

— He orders his father to fight the coming of death and instead cling to life. This is *repeated* several times, acting as a powerful *refrain* which gives the order an emotionally-charged urgency.

'Old age should burn and rave at close of day; Rage, rage against the dying of the light.'

— Death is seen as a painful, emotional event as he states '**old age should burn**' and that elderly people should '**rage, rage against the dying of the light**'.

— The *words* '**burn**' and '**rage**' suggest a searing pain and a fury, perhaps the pain of the dying man who realises that life and all its opportunities are almost over.

— Life is linked with '**light**' and its associations with hope and optimism, whereas death is seen as '**the close of day**', with darkness and finality.

'Though wise men at their end know dark is right, Because their words had forked no lightning they Do not go gentle into that good night.'

— '**wise men**' acknowledge that death is a natural ending to our lives.

- The simple *phrase* with the *monosyllabic words* **'dark is right'** captures this understanding that death comes as the inevitable and inescapable conclusion.

- Men who have lived a long life and acquired wisdom understand this, and yet they still fight the final ending.

- This is because they know they have not achieved what they wanted from life. The *metaphor* **'their words had forked no lightning'** captures how their lives have been uninspiring and unimpactful. The idea of **'lightning'** suggests a huge flash of powerful light and electricity that illuminates the sky in a spectacular way, which implies that we all have a desire to light up the world with our ideas and actions.

- Yet these men are at the end of their lives and have not managed to do this. There is a sense of regret and failure at missed opportunities, and therefore an unwillingness to accept death.

'Wild men who caught and sang the sun in flight,
And learn, too late, they grieved it on its way'

- Each *stanza* gives the reader an example of old men who fight death as they have regrets.

- This *stanza* comments on **'wild men'** who seem to be daring, adventurous men who lived life to the full. They are possibly men who have lived their lives indulging in pleasure: living to excess, drinking and partying.

- The *metaphor* **'caught and sang the sun in flight'** suggests they held onto the sun, harnessing its power.

- Yet the sun is now leaving the sky and, **'too late'**, they realise that they will die and that they passed their lives pursuing pleasure.

'And you, my father, there on the sad height,
Curse, bless, me now with your fierce tears, I pray.'

- In this *stanza*, there is a shift in the pattern of the lines to ABAA as the *villanelle* comes to an end. This echoes a shift from the general to the very personal as Thomas now addresses **'my father'** directly using the *personal pronoun* **'you'**.

- There is an emotional conflict which is established with the *oppositional verbs* **'curse'** and **'bless'**; the speaker seems desperate to keep his father with him on any terms.

- At the end, the *refrain* **'Do not go gentle into that good night./ Rage, rage against the dying of the light'** is *repeated* for the final time. The relentless *repetition* perhaps shows the inevitability of death and how it cannot be avoided: that we all have to accept in the end our own mortality.

Remember
by Christina Rossetti

'Remember' is a poem about grief and remembrance written from the perspective of the person who is dying. The speaker asks their loved one to remember them, but at the same time, to not be consumed by despair.

Structure and Form: The poem takes the form of a **Petrarchan sonnet**, which was a form of love poetry developed in the 14th century. The fourteen lines of the **sonnet** are separated into an **octave**, in which a theme of conflict is introduced, followed by a **sestet**, which provides a resolution. The **octave** has a regular ABBA **rhyme scheme** but the **sestet**, signified by the **volta** (the change in argument) is more varied. In 'Remember', Rossetti uses a CDDECE **rhyme scheme** at this point to represent the change in her feelings.

'Remember me when I am gone away,
Gone far away into the silent land;'

— This poem is significant because of its simplicity of language and its honesty. The poet does not become overly emotional as seen in other Victorian **eulogies**.

— The use of the *imperative verb* **'Remember'** is clear and direct as if the speaker is talking to a loved one who she fears will forget her once they are no longer able to communicate.

— The use of *anadiplosis* – '**I am gone away,/ Gone far away ..**' emphasises the permanency of death and the breaking of the connection between them.

— Death is metaphorically described as a journey into a distant and '**silent land**'. The speaker will be voiceless in death and therefore has no power to keep their relationship alive.

'When you can no more hold me by the hand,
Nor I half turn to go yet turning stay.'

— The **sonnet** uses **iambic pentameter**, which is a series of unstressed and stressed **syllables** often associated with a heartbeat. By using this specific **metre**, the reader can assume that this is a personal message to a loved one.

— The **verb 'stay'** reflects a return to a previous rhyme **'away'**, which echoes the meaning of the line as the speaker talks about the ability she has had in life to walk away then return. The memory of her will be the only way in which she will be able to return after death.

— The poet moves from the lack of communication in the first two lines to the lack of physical contact after death. The **alliterative** '**h**' sounds in '**hold me by the hand**' form an aural connection between the lovers as well as alluding to a physical one in their lives.

'Only remember me; you understand
It will be late to counsel then or pray.'

— The **adverb** '**Only**' has a number of alternative interpretations. The speaker could be asking her lover to not remember anyone else but her; she could be suggesting that she doesn't want him to do anything else, just remember her; or he should remember just her and not any disputes or conflicts they may have had.

— The insistence of the command is important and the directness of the **declarative** '**you understand…**' implies that the loved one may not fully accept what is happening.

'Yet if you should forget me for a while
And afterwards remember, do not grieve:'

— The **volta** begins on line 9 with the **conjunction** '**Yet**', which introduces the surprising twist in the argument. Up to this point the speaker has asked for her loved one to remember her – now the **imperative** '**do not grieve**' seems to imply the reverse.

— The **rhyme scheme** changes in this section of the poem (the **sestet**) to become more irregular as the poet faces the reality that her loved one may forget her for a while. Grief and mourning do not follow a regular pattern but comes and goes sporadically as life goes on for the mourner.

'Better by far you should forget and smile
Than that you should remember and be sad.'

— The final lines of the poem encapsulate the speaker's message: that it is better if her loved one is happy in his future life rather than grieve and fall into despair.

— **Parallelism** is used to emphasise the different situations left for the speaker's loved one. The **repetitive structure** and use of **antithesis** reinforces the differences between the two scenarios. He must '**forget**' and '**smile**' rather than '**remember**' and be '**sad**'.

— Employing the **second-person** and the **modal verb** '**should**' reflect the forceful voice of the speaker as she expresses the desire for him to be happy.

— The message seems somewhat contradictory since the first **octave** was spent demanding that her loved one remember her. The final **sestet** adds a more realistic and compassionate hope that a trace of her will always be with him but that he should not allow her death to be a burden he carries forever.

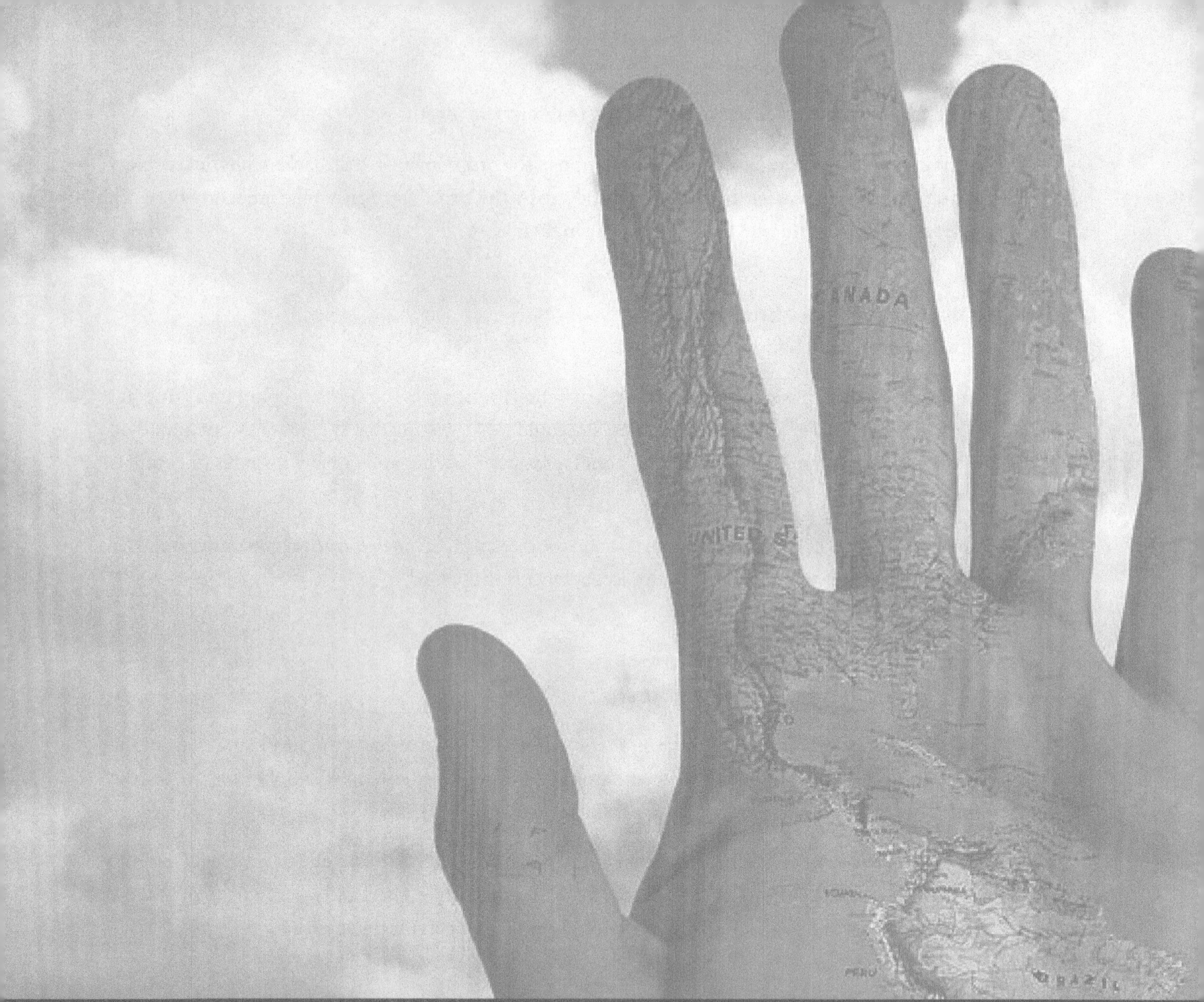
ANADA
UNITED
PERU

PART II

Exam Success: Revision Guide for IGCSE Edexcel Poetry Anthology

Alison Goodall and Janet Oliver

Compare how the writers present the importance of memory in 'Piano' and 'Poem at Thirty-Nine'.

Piano

The title of the poem relates to an object that is associated with nostalgic childhood memories of Lawrence's mother playing and singing. The poem has a regretful mood.

Both poets show how memories of parents are important to them. Nostalgia is tinged with regret and sadness.

Poem at Thirty-Nine

The title refers to the age when Walker wrote her poem, reminiscing about her late father and the qualities that she admired. The memories are filled with a sense of loss.

Written in three *quatrains* consisting of two *rhyming couplets*, which create a clear structure to the memories that he recounts. The irregular line lengths and *rhythms* reflect the movement between past and present.

Both poems use irregular line lengths and rhythms to convey the way in which memories are fragmentary. However, Lawrence uses rhyming couplets to echo the very fixed and specific memory from his childhood.

The poem is written in *free verse* with no specific *rhyme scheme* or *rhythm*. This creates a *stream of consciousness* reflecting the way memories ebb and flow. *Internal rhyme* reflects the connection between father and daughter.

A soft and intimate mood is created: **'Softly, in the dusk…'** Past and present blurs like the merging of night and day. Personal pronoun **'me'** creates a connection between music and a very personal and significant memory.

Both speakers express a sense of loss which takes them back into the past to remember a parent who has passed away.

The tone is mournful and highly emotional. The declarative **'How I miss my father'** creates an opening to the past and all that the poet **'miss'** (es) about her father. The feeling is unapologetic and ever-present.

40 | *Exam Success*

The speaker's memories are intrinsically linked to music - a memory so significant to him, it is triggered by events in the present. **'In the boom of the tingling strings'** he is literally and metaphorically immersed in music. Music has had a profound and long-lasting effect on him.	**Memories are triggered by events in the speakers' present day lives. Both speakers have been profoundly affected by the past.**	Food and cooking are used as a motif to symbolise the warmth and vitality she remembers in her father. His love of cooking has affected the way in which she uses ingredients as well as how she lives her life: **'seasoning none of my life/ the same way twice;'** referring, metaphorically, to her carefree approach to life.
The speaker yearns so much for the comfort of **'the old Sunday evenings at home'** that he feels his **'manhood is cast/ Down'.** His memories are impacting his adult self as any protective shield of masculinity is broken down and overcome by the **'flood'** of his childhood recollections. The *noun* **'flood'** implies that the emotions have overwhelmed him.	**Both poets focus on how memories have impacted their adult selves; however Walker has been inspired to move forward with her life, whilst Lawrence has a yearning to stay in the past.**	Walker used the memories she had of her austere childhood to spur her on to **'escape'** using **'bits of paper'**. *Metaphorically*, the **'bits of paper'** could relate to Walker's own writing and her success as a famous author and poet. The *varied line lengths* and *enjambment* highlight the way in which Walker's thoughts ebb and flow like a tide of memories.
The speaker is unwillingly pulled back into the past - the memory is warm and intimate but the longing he feels for a return to this state is unbearable. The *personification* of music as something that **'betrays'** the speaker furthers the idea that music is somehow treacherous and deceitful: the speaker is tricked into returning to his childhood memory.	**Both poets are pulled back into their past when their thoughts focus on a particular person. However, for Lawrence this is a reluctant process, whilst Walker is happy to celebrate her father's life.**	Walker has fond memories of her father who **'cooked like a person/ dancing/ in a yoga meditation'**. The *antithesis* of **'dancing'** and **'meditation'** highlights the unique qualities of her father: he is capable of both joyful exuberance as well as reflection and spirituality. Whilst others are quiet and subdued, he is **'dancing'**.
At the end of the poem, the speaker is left emotionally drained as his adult rationality is stripped away in favour of the raw reaction of a child. The *simile* **'I weep like a child for the past'** exposes the power that music can have on the listener: it can be both uplifting and destructive.	**Both poets see memory as something that can be painful. They both show regret that the people who have died can only be a part of their lives through memories.**	The memories of her father are joyful but there is a tone of sadness. **'He would have grown/ to admire…'** who she has become. The *modal verb* **'would'** shows a possible disconnection in their relationship. She doesn't know for sure how he felt, indicating a lack of communication, or a lack of time to convince him of her positive qualities.

Compare how the writers present the importance of memory in 'Piano' and 'Poem at Thirty-Nine'.

Both 'Piano' and 'Poem at Thirty-Nine' (which are widely thought to be autobiographical) focus on the significance of childhood memories and their impact on the daily lives of the writers. Both poets show how memories of parents are important to them, but nostalgia is tinged with regret and sadness. Lawrence explores how memories of childhood bring both joy and longing for a world to which we can never return whilst Walker wrote her poem, reminiscing about her late father and the qualities that she admired. Written in *free verse* using *irregular line lengths* and a loose structure to represent how memories drift in and out of the writer's mind, the overall effect is a *stream of consciousness* that allows us to see snippets of her father's life. However, Lawrence's poem focuses on one specific memory using *rhyming couplets* to provide a clear structure and a sense of predictability, which is somehow comforting.

The memories of both speakers begin with a sense of loss which takes them back into the past to remember a parent who has passed away. 'Piano' begins with the speaker listening to a woman singing: **'Softly, in the dusk, a woman is singing to me'.** The sound transports him back to a childhood memory of sitting at his mother's feet under the piano as she plays and sings. The *adverbial phrase* in the first line of the poem creates a warm and intimate feeling: the use of *sibilance* giving the line a soft and seductive tone. The setting is dusk, a magical time when the distinction between day and night becomes blurred and obscure. *Symbolically,* this alludes to the blurring of past and present, adulthood and childhood that the speaker is about to experience. Similarly, Walker's poem opens with a quiet and gentle, yet highly emotional mood with the declarative **'How I miss my father'** creating an opening to the past and all that the poet **'miss'** (es) about her father. The feeling is unapologetic and ever-present. Using the *first person* **'I'** and the *possessive pronoun* **'my'** shows that this is an intensely personal poem in a similar way to Lawrence's use of the pronoun **'me'** to end the opening line of 'Piano'.

Both speakers have been profoundly affected by their past experiences, and the memories they have provide a continuous link to that past. Lawrence's memories are intrinsically linked to music - a memory so significant to him, it is triggered by events in the present. **'In the boom of the tingling strings'** he is literally and metaphorically immersed in music. *Sensory language* including the *onomatopoeic* **'boom'** recreates a world where music had such an intense and long-lasting effect on him, the **'tingling strings'** an extension of his own heightened sensibilities. For Walker, it is food and cooking which are used as motifs to symbolise the warmth and vitality she remembers in her father. His love of cooking has affected the way in which she uses ingredients as well as how she lives her life: **'seasoning none of my life/ the same way twice;'** referring, metaphorically, to her carefree approach to life. **'Seasoning'** is used to enhance and boost the flavour of food. By using the *verb* to describe how she approaches life, Walker is suggesting that she has emulated her father's joy of creating new flavours as well as enjoying new experiences both culinary and in life itself.

Both poets focus on how memories have impacted their adult selves; however Walker has been inspired to move forward with her life, whilst Lawrence has a yearning to stay in the past. Here the speaker yearns so much for the comfort of **'the old Sunday evenings at home'** that he feels his **'manhood is cast down'**. His memories are impacting his adult self as any protective shield of masculinity is broken down and overcome by the **'flood'** of his childhood recollections. The *noun* **'flood'** implies that the emotions have overwhelmed him. Walker does not dwell in the past like Lawrence. She used the memories she had of her austere childhood to spur her on to **'escape'** using **'bits of paper'**. *Metaphorically*, the **'bits of paper'** could relate to Walker's own writing and her success as a famous author and poet. The *varied line lengths* and *enjambment* highlight the way in which Walker's thoughts ebb and flow like a tide of memories.

As well as the positive experiences of remembering loved ones, both poets see memory as something that can be painful. They both show regret that the people who have died can only be a part of their lives through memories. At the end of 'Piano', the speaker is left emotionally drained as his adult rationality is stripped away in favour of the raw reaction of a child. The *simile* **'I weep like a child for the past'** exposes the power that memories can have on the individual: they can be both uplifting and destructive. Similarly, the memories in 'Poem at Thirty-Nine' are joyful but there is also a tone of sadness. The poet reflects on how her father **'would have grown/ to admire … cooking, writing, chopping wood/ staring into the fire.'** The items in the list all signify something she has learnt from her father: the **'cooking'** represents warmth and generosity; **'writing'** has resulted in financial independence; **'chopping wood'** shows her self-sufficiency; and the final act of **'staring into the fire'** implies a reflective and contemplative soul, mirroring the balance that her father demonstrated through his life. However, the *modal verb* **'would'** shows a possible disconnection in their relationship. She doesn't know for sure how he felt, indicating a lack of communication, or a lack of time to convince him of her positive qualities. Like Lawrence, Walker is left to reflect on the significance of her memories and how they impact her life in the present.

Compare how the writers present childhood experiences in 'Half-past Two' and 'Hide and Seek'.

Hide and Seek		Half-past Two
The title refers to a familiar childhood game suggesting happy times. The game begins with great excitement but ends with disappointment and loneliness. 	**Both poems focus on childhood experiences; however whilst one is an enjoyable game, the other is a punishment.**	The title is a specific time related to an after-school detention implying an upsetting experience. The time is significant to the teacher but the child has no concept of what it means. 
Free verse and a lack of *stanza* breaks create a *stream of consciousness*. Several *rhyming couplets* are used for cohesion whilst *direct speech* and *imperatives* suggest nervous tension.	**Both poets use free verse to create conversational tones that suggest retellings of childhood experiences.**	*Free verse* with the lack of a regular *rhyme scheme* and *rhythm* creates a conversational *tone*. Eleven *stanzas* give a structure to events, and irregular line lengths, including some longer lines suggest an elongation of time.
'I'm ready! Come and find me! - clear, confident voice suggests an expert at the game. *Exclamative sentences* create an air of excitement and anticipation. Child is taunting the seekers. He feels superior and in control. But who is the **'you'** that the speaker is addressing? 	**Whilst the voice in 'Hide and Seek' is confident and controlled, the child in 'Half-past Two' is unsure and nervous.**	'And She said he'd done Something Very Wrong' - uncertain and nervous voice. The *capitalisation* of the *adverb*, 'Very' and the *adjective*, 'Wrong' indicate the angry tone of the teacher and emphasise the words imprinted on the boy's memory. Capitalisation of **'She'** indicates authority and superiority. 

44 | Exam Success

The boy waits in the shed. At first protective and comforting: '**The sacks… smell like the seaside**', but later cold and uncomfortable. *Pre-modifiers* '**dark damp**' convey a more oppressive and claustrophobic atmosphere to his hiding place. *Synaesthesia* blends literal and the metaphorical worlds together as the hider sits in the '**salty dark**.'

Both personas remember the time spent waiting, not knowing when it would end.

The young boy could not read a clock - entered into a timeless world of waiting in the classroom. Surreal experience. A vivid sensory description of the classroom, a strange otherworldly experience: '**smell of old chrysanthemums**'

'**he'd escaped for ever**' - freedom and liberation from the structured school day.

Persona is seemingly in control of events: '**Don't breathe. Don't move. Stay dumb. Hide in your blindness**'. Series of *imperative verbs* emphasised by the *anaphora* creates drama. '**Blindness**' refers to lack of mature understanding.

Both poets explore an event that highlights a lack of understanding of the adult world.

'**He knew the clockface, the little eyes/ And two long legs for walking**'. *Alliteration* and *assonance* used to create a feeling of time extending. *Personification* of the clock's features highlight the boy's childlike perception of time.

Poem ends with a *rhetorical question*, adding a tentative, uncertain tone. '**But where are they who sought you?**' Whilst the hider has been feeling smug and secure in his victory, the seekers have lost interest and gone home. The boy may have won the game but in doing so, he has lost himself.

Both poets point to the lesson that can be learnt from the experiences although it is unclear whether or not the child in 'Hide and Seek' changed as a result.

Time is *personified* as we are shown the profound effect this childhood experience had on him. '**time hides tick-less waiting to be born.**' He has '**never forgot**' how he entered a world where time did not exist, held in a state before the clock began to rule his life.

Revision Guide for IGCSE Edexcel Poetry Anthology | 45

Compare how the writers present childhood experiences in 'Half-past Two' and 'Hide and Seek'.

Whilst both 'Half-past Two' and 'Hide and Seek' focus on childhood experiences, one explores the excitement and anticipation of an enjoyable game, whilst the other is centred round a detention given to a young child. Scannell uses a second-person narrative voice to give advice on how to win a game of hide-and-seek. However, the poem is also an *extended metaphor*, highlighting the dangers of socially isolating oneself and how life's seeming victories can lead to disappointment and loneliness. In Fanthorpe's poem a young boy has misbehaved at school and his teacher has put him in detention until **'half-past two'**. Having no concept of how to read a clock, the boy enters into a mysterious world where time has no meaning. Both experiences have profound effects on the children involved and serve as life lessons to us all.

Both poets use *free verse* to create conversational tones that suggest retellings of childhood experiences. 'Hide and Seek' is written as a *stream of consciousness*: the twenty-seven lines, which are undivided by any *stanza* breaks incorporate *direct speech* and a series of *imperatives* to create an excitable and nervous tension, echoing the feelings of the child hiding in the shed. Unlike Scannell's poem, 'Half-past Two' has eleven *tercets*, which give structure to the memory. Line lengths are irregular, some only containing six *syllables*, whilst others contain as many as thirteen. These lines create the sense of time becoming elongated as the boy sits waiting for his detention to end. Both poets use the structure of their poems to reflect the passing of time and the feelings of the children who are trapped in its grip.

Due to the nature of the childhood experience the voices of the two personas are very different. Whilst the child in 'Hide and Seek' is confident and controlled, the boy in 'Half-past Two' is unsure and nervous. The *capitalisation* of the *adverb*, 'Very' and the *adjective*, 'Wrong' in the line **'And She said he'd done Something Very Wrong'** indicate the angry tone of the teacher and emphasise the words imprinted on the boy's memory. His experience from the start is seen from his position of inferiority in the face of a superior authority emphasised by the capitalisation of the pronoun **'She'**. The child in 'Hide and Seek', however, is very much in control. The series of short *imperative sentences* that open the poem create a clear and confident voice. The child considers himself an expert in the game and the instruction to **'Call loud'** conveys a sense that the child has no concern at being caught. *Exclamative sentences* **'I'm ready! Come and find me!'** create an air of excitement and anticipation as if the child is taunting the seekers, safe in the knowledge that he will not be found. But who is the **'you'** that the speaker is addressing? The voice could be an *internal monologue*, a guide created by the child and acting as a fellow conspirator in this game of hide and seek. Or the speaker could be addressing **'you'** the reader, giving clear instructions on how to play and win the game. Whether the speaker is addressing himself or the reader, the outcome is the same. The game ends with disappointment and loss.

Although the circumstances of their childhood experiences are very different, both personas remember the time spent waiting, not knowing when it would end. In Scannell's poem, the recurring *image* of the sea and in particular the sandbags behind which the boy is hiding, initially convey a feeling of protection and familiarity. The seaside has positive connotations, of wide expanses of sand, salty sea air and childhood holidays. The boy immerses himself in the image of this environment to deflect his thoughts from the darkness of the shed. Scannell uses *synaesthesia* to blend the literal and the metaphorical worlds together as the hider sits in the '**salty dark**'. However, as time goes on and the boy is still undiscovered, his environment becomes cold and uncomfortable. The *pre-modifiers* '**dark damp**' convey a more oppressive and claustrophobic atmosphere to his hiding place as the feelings of loneliness and isolation replace his initial excitement. The young boy in 'Half-past Two' enters a similarly perpetual world of waiting, although his situation is not self-imposed. The *vivid sensory description* of the classroom brings the reader into the timeless world he has entered as he has no idea when, or if, his normal life will ever resume. The flowers are '**old**' and the sound of his hangnail is '**silent**'. These *adjectives* serve to recreate a strange, almost otherworldly atmosphere where time is suspended. The *verb* '**escaped**' together with the *intensifier* '**for ever**' creates a sense of freedom and liberation from the strict authoritarian order of the school day. Like the child in the shed, he is in a period of stasis, waiting for time to begin again.

These situations that the children find themselves in highlight a lack of understanding of the adult world. The boy in the classroom has no concept of how to read a clock so he is unable to engage with the adult notion of time. His perception of time was linked to certain events like getting up, going to school and even kissing grandma. The *personification* of the clock's features highlight the boy's childlike view of time as he imagines the hour and minute hands '**walking**' around the face which looks over him with '**little eyes**'. *Alliteration* and *assonance* in '**long legs for walking**' are used to create a feeling of time extending, as it must have felt to the young boy in the schoolroom. Similarly, in 'Hide and Seek' the persona loses all perception of time as he waits for the seekers to discover him. However, he feels very much in control of his situation as he reminds himself '**Don't breathe. Don't move. Stay dumb. Hide in your blindness**'. As the boy waits apprehensively in his hiding place, he hears the voices of the seekers coming closer. The series of *imperative verbs* emphasised by the *anaphora* used at the start of the line create drama and tension as the words act as a warning that his wait may be over. However, there is another, more adult voice, which is perhaps commenting on the child's immature feeling of superiority. Literally, the command to '**Stay dumb**' is referring to his need for silence but *metaphorically*, the speaker could be commenting on the act of socially isolating oneself as foolish.

Both poets point to the lessons that can be learnt from the experiences, although it is unclear whether or not the child in '**Hide and Seek**' changed as a result. The poem ends with a *rhetorical question*, adding a tentative, uncertain tone. '**But where are they who sought you?**' Whilst the hider has been feeling smug and secure in his victory, the seekers have lost interest and gone home. The boy may have won the game but in doing so, he has lost himself. Meanwhile, the boy in Fanthorpe's poem is discovered - by the teacher - and released. Time is *personified* as we are shown the profound effect this childhood experience had on him: '**time hides tick-less waiting to be born.**' He has '**never forgot**' how he entered a world where time did not exist, held in a state before the clock began to rule his life. Both children experienced a period when they waited to be found, where they existed in isolation. For both it was a lesson they will not forget.

Compare how the writers present relationships in 'Sonnet 116' and 'My Last Duchess'.

Sonnet 116		My Last Duchess
The title reflects the poem's place in the chronology of Shakepeare's 154 sonnets. Sonnet 116 is thought to have been written for a mysterious young man known as Fair Youth.	**Both poems focus on a romantic commitment. However, one is a more generalised, philosophical notion of love.**	The title sets the context of the poem: written about the Duke of Ferrara and his wife, Lucia, it implies the unimportance of this duchess. The possessive pronoun 'My' suggests the Duke's control.
Sonnet form: fourteen lines of *iambic pentameter* divided into three *quatrains* and a *rhyming couplets*. The rigid structure implies the unwavering nature of love.	**Both poets use strict rhythms and rhyme schemes to show strong feelings.**	*Dramatic monologue*: no *stanza* breaks. Only the Duke's voice is heard. *Enjambment* and *iambic pentameter* give a conversational *tone* and show he is in complete control.
A relationship based on equality: '**the marriage of true minds**'. The *pre-modifier* '**true**' suggests a marriage based on an equal understanding of love: a permanent and enduring state which does not alter as the relationship progresses.	**Whilst one poet explores equality within a relationship, the other focuses on a dominant and controlling husband.**	A relationship based on domination and control - even in death. '**none puts by/ The curtain I have drawn for you, but I**'. *Syntactical placement* of '**but I**' emphasises it is he who has the final command.

48 | Exam Success

The persona places his trust in the concept of love: **'O no, it is an ever-fixed mark/'** By comparing love to a star, which guides sailors as they navigate rough seas, he suggests that love is a constant point of reference and something that can be trusted.	**The speakers place their trust in different things - the abstract nature of love versus the materialistic value of wealth and status.**	The duke places value on status to impress his wife: **'my gift of a nine-hundred-years-old name'**. The *tone* is of arrogant pride in the fact he can trace his ancestry back so far. The use of the *noun* **'gift'** shows how he chooses to share this status.
The persona talks of love being unwavering, and unchanged by time: **'Love's not Time's fool'**. The speaker suggests that Love is not deceived by Time. Love does not change even if beauty is destroyed because love is of **'true minds'** and does not depend on physical attributes.	**The speakers have different views on the longevity of love. One is adamant that love endures whilst the other sees love as fickle.**	The duke is suspicious of his wife and doubts her fidelity. **'her looks went everywhere'**.

The Duke clearly disapproves of his wife's actions. There is a suggestion that she wasn't aloof (superior) enough, and also that she was flirtatious/unfaithful. |
| Love is seen as something which continues beyond death to the end of time. **'Love…bears it out even to the edge of doom.'** The *abstract noun* **'doom'** represents a catastrophic time when all life ends. Love will only die when all life is extinguished. | **Both poets explore the nature of love after death.** | The speaker sees the relationship as something he can end permanently: **'I gave commands;/ Then all smiles stopped together.'** The sly **sibilance** **'smiles stopped'** highlights the sinister nature of the killing of the Duchess. |

Revision Guide for IGCSE Edexcel Poetry Anthology | 49

Compare how the writers present relationships in 'Sonnet 116' and 'My Last Duchess'.

In both 'Sonnet 116' and 'My Last Duchess' the poets present ideas about relationships and the emotions that can be evoked when one develops a close attachment; however, the sentiments involved are very different. 'Sonnet 116' describes the enduring nature of true love as something which is fixed and unwavering, unchanged by time or circumstances, whereas 'My Last Duchess' explores the possessive and controlling relationship between a sixteenth-century Italian Duke and his late wife. Written in the traditional form of love poetry, Shakespeare's **sonnet** features a rigid **rhyme scheme** and **rhythm**, which perhaps reflects the poet's message regarding the unchangeable and constant idea of love. Even though the speaker's voice is the only one heard, the poem explores the equality inherent in a loving relationship. In contrast, the **dramatic monologue** employed by Browning to explore the Duke of Ferrara's relationship, conveys the complete control the latter has over those around him. No other voice is permitted to speak and the feelings he conveys to his listener, the envoy, are entirely egotistical and self-serving.

So, whilst one poet explores equality within a relationship, the other focuses on a dominant and controlling husband. Even in the title of the poem, 'My Last Duchess' the Duke is portrayed as a man who likes to control others. The **possessive pronoun 'my'** shows that his wife belongs to him; he sees her as a possession, one of many that he collects. He defines her as **'last Duchess'** which implies she is one in a long list of wives, unimportant in herself. In life, the Duchess is powerless in the relationship and once she is dead, the Duke has absolute control over who can look at her. The Duke is the one who chooses when the curtain covering her portrait is open or closed, as shown when he declares that **'none puts by/ The curtain I have drawn for you, but I'**. His control is also seen in the structure of these lines: the **enjambment** here shows how he controls the flow of lines and the **syntactical placement** of **'but I'** at the end of the line emphasises it is he who has the final command. In contrast to this, the speaker in 'Sonnet 116' begins the poem with an echo of the marriage vows as he declares **'Let me not to the marriage of true minds/ Admit impediments'**. Unlike the jealous Duke in 'My Last Duchess' the speaker believes that nothing should stand in the way of two people who are truly in love. The **verb 'admit'** implies that true love will never allow anything to change its course. The union that is described is one of **'true minds'**. The **pre-modifier 'true'** could suggest a marriage based on an equal understanding of love: a permanent and enduring state which does not alter as the relationship progresses.

Although both poems explore the idea of commitment within relationships, the speakers place value on different things within those relationships. The speaker in 'Sonnet 116' places his faith in love, and trusts in the whole notion of an enduring passion, which will remain constant - **'an ever-fixed mark'**. In the Elizabethan era, mariners would depend on the North Star, the **'ever-fixed mark'**, to navigate their way across the ocean. The **metaphor** confirms the speaker's view of love. By comparing love to a star, which guides sailors as they navigate rough seas, he suggests that love is a constant point of reference and something that can be trusted, even if all around you is turmoil. ***Iambic pentameter*** is used to provide a smooth and fluent rhythm, reflecting the way that love can guide you smoothly through life's difficulties. However, the Duke places value, not on any emotional union but on materialism and status. He feels that his wife should show him the proper respect for '**my gift of a nine-hundred-years-old name**'. The use of the ***noun*** '**gift**' shows how he chooses to share this status as he has the power to bestow his high-class name on his wife. The ***tone*** is of arrogant pride in the fact he can trace his ancestry back so far- his family has held power for almost a millennia. Whilst he will remove any impediments to his power and egotism even if it means sacrificing the relationship with his former Duchess, the speaker in 'Sonnet 116' believes that love can overcome any obstacle.

The speakers have different views on the longevity of love and relationships. One is adamant that love endures whilst the other sees love as fickle. In 'Sonnet 116' '**Love**' is ***personified*** as it is not '**Time's fool**'. The ***possessive noun*** suggests that Time tries to make an idiot out of '**Love**' by ruining the physical appearance of the loved one and thus destroying the concept of enduring love. However, the speaker suggests that Love does not change even if beauty is destroyed because love is of '**true minds**' and does not depend on physical attributes. So love is enduring, constant and everlasting. However, the Duke sees love as fickle. He is suspicious of his wife and doubts her fidelity: '**her looks went everywhere**'. The Duchess does not share this love of status; she places her value on natural pleasures: watching the sunset, '**the dropping of the daylight**', riding her '**white mule**', eating '**cherries**'. There is a suggestion that she wasn't aloof enough, and also that she was flirtatious. The Duke clearly disapproves of his wife's actions and he is suspicious of her behaviour. For the Duke of Ferrara, love is not the overriding factor in the relationship. He demands absolute loyalty, subservience and obedience as opposed to the equality seen in 'Sonnet 116'. The consequences of the Duke's perverse view of love and relationships are dramatic and severe.

Indeed, the Duke sees the relationship as something he can end permanently: '**I gave commands; / Then all smiles stopped together.**' The authoritative ***tone*** of '**I gave commands**' is highlighted by the ***pause*** at the end of the line and emphasises what comes after: the vile consequences of these commands, his wife's murder. The sly ***sibilance*** '**smiles stopped**' highlights the sinister nature of the killing of the Duchess. It is interesting that the Duke says '**all smiles stopped**'. The ***determiner*** '**all**' could perhaps suggest that his own smiles stopped as well. It is possible that he did have feelings for her after all, and that his desire for power over his wife made him go too far - a decision that he then regrets. In contrast, the speaker in 'Sonnet 116' regards a loving relationship as something that continues beyond death to the end of time: '**Love…bears it out even to the edge of doom.**' The ***abstract noun*** '**doom**' represents a catastrophic time when all life ends. Love will only die when all life is extinguished. The poem ends with the declaration that '**If this be error**' then '**I never writ, nor no man ever lov'd.**' The ***subordinating conjunction***, '**If**' is used to introduce the ***conditional clause***, but the speaker is not providing a counter-argument. Rather, he is summarising his impassioned declaration: if he is wrong about love then he states that he never wrote anything and no man was ever in love. In other words, he is certain of his argument. In fact, both the Duke and the speaker in 'Sonnet 116' are certain of their beliefs and are dogmatic in their delivery. They both convey their thoughts with conviction although one with much more optimism.

Compare how the writers present ideas about death and mourning in 'Remember' and 'Do not go gentle'.

Remember		Do not go gentle
The poem's title **'Remember'** takes the form of an *imperative verb*, giving a clear instruction to a lover from the perspective of the speaker who is dying.	**In both 'Remember' and 'Do not go gentle' the poets present advice to a persona who is facing the death of a loved one but the perspectives are very different.**	The title of the poem uses the *imperative form* to convey Thomas' message, as he urges his father, and, perhaps, the reader, to resist death and hold onto life.
The poem takes the form of a *Petrarchan sonnet.* The fourteen lines of the *sonnet* are separated into an *octave*, in which the speaker urges her loved one to remember her after death, followed by a *sestet*, when her thoughts change to her loved one's future happiness. The regularity of the form suggests the containment of her feelings in a difficult situation.	**Both poems include a change in the advice given, which is reflected in the structure and form.**	The poem takes the form of a *villanelle*, a nineteen-line poem that follows a *regular rhyme scheme.* This strict form, combined with the ten-syllable *rhythm* and regular three-line *stanzas*, suggests that Thomas is using this rigid pattern to perhaps contain his grief at the prospect of his father's approaching death. The last stanza is a direct address to his father.
Death is a permanent loss which is an accepted fact of life. Death is metaphorically described as a journey into a distant and **'silent land'**. The speaker is accepting of her fate and just wants her loved one to remember her once she has gone. The use of *anadiplosis* – **'I am gone away,/ Gone far away ..'** emphasises the permanency of death and the breaking of the connection between them.	**Both poets see death as a permanent loss but the poets have different views about how one should approach it.**	Death is a permanent loss and something that should be fought against. Death is seen as a painful, emotional event as he states **'old age should burn'** and that elderly people should **'rage, rage against the dying of the light'**. The *words* **'burn'** and **'rage'** suggest a searing pain and a fury, perhaps the pain of the dying man who realises that life and all its opportunities are almost over.

52 | *Exam Success*

Death brings great change.

After death, there will be no more physical contact between the lovers to keep their relationship alive. It is only the memory which must survive: **'you can no more hold me by the hand … stay'**. The speaker reminds us that death is a permanent state and that there is no returning. The *alliterative* **'h'** sounds create an aural as well as a physical connection which will be lost. The tone is regretful and mournful.

Both poets explore how death brings regret and a sense of loss. Life's experiences are over and there is no turning back. No second chances.

Death brings great change.

The poet includes examples of those who fight death as they have regrets about their lives: **'Wild men who caught and sang the sun in flight'** now **'grieved it on its way'**. The *metaphor* relates to the pleasure-seekers who harnessed the power of the sun but now realise it is leaving the sky and regret their hedonistic pursuits. They have no chance to properly appreciate life's opportunities so, according to the speaker, should rage against its ending.

Death is a personal experience.

The final lines of the poem encapsulate the speaker's message: that it is better if her loved one is happy in his future life rather than grieve and fall into despair. *Parallelism* is used to emphasise the different situations left for the speaker's loved one. The *repetitive structure* and use of *antithesis* reinforces the differences between the two scenarios. He must **'forget'** and **'smile'** rather than **'remember'** and be **'sad'**.

Death and mourning are very personal. Both poets give specific advice on how to react to death but from different perspectives.

Death is a personal experience.

The shift in the pattern of the lines to ABAA, as the *villanelle* comes to an end, echoes a shift from the general to the very personal as Thomas now addresses **'my father'** directly using the *personal pronoun* **'you'**. There is an emotional conflict which is established with the **oppositional verbs** in the line **'Curse, bless, me now'**; the speaker seems desperate to keep his father with him on any terms.

Abstract nouns **'darkness'** and **'corruption'** are used to describe the **'silent land'** previously referred to and seem to add a more sober view of death. The speaker is sightless as well as voiceless in the other world, and she touches on the reality of death when referencing the decay of the physical state to which the body will succumb.

In both poems, death is seen as a place of silence and darkness after the light of life has been extinguished.

At the end, the *refrain* **'Do not go gentle into that good night,/ Rage, rage against the dying of the light'** is *repeated* for the final time. The relentless repetition perhaps shows the inevitability of death and how it cannot be avoided. Life is linked with **'light'** and its associations with hope and optimism, whereas death is seen as **'the close of day'**, with darkness and finality.

Revision Guide for IGCSE Edexcel Poetry Anthology | 53

Compare how the writers present ideas about death and mourning in 'Remember' and 'Do not go gentle'.

In both 'Remember' and 'Do not go gentle' the poets present advice to a persona who is facing death but the perspectives are very different. Whilst Thomas urges his father, and, perhaps, the reader, to resist death and hold onto life, Rossetti's sonnet is written from the perspective of the person who is dying and reveals a greater acceptance of death. The speaker asks their loved one to remember them, but at the same time, to not be consumed by despair unlike Thomas who insists that his father rage at the prospect of death. Both titles adopt the **imperative form** to indicate the demands of the speaker. '**Remember**' is clear and direct as if the speaker is talking to a loved one who she fears will forget her once they are no longer able to communicate. The **tone** is quiet and acquiescent. However, '**Do not go gentle**' whilst also clear and direct, suggests a more confrontational and defiant mood. He orders his father to fight the coming of death and instead cling to life. This is **repeated** several times, acting as a powerful **refrain** which gives the order an emotionally-charged urgency.

Both poems include a change in the advice given to the respective listeners, which is reflected in the structure and form. 'Remember' takes the form of a **Petrarchan sonnet**. The fourteen lines of the **sonnet** are separated into an **octave**, in which the speaker urges her loved one to remember her after death, followed by a **sestet**, when her thoughts change to her loved one's future happiness. Indeed, the message seems somewhat contradictory since the first **octave** was spent demanding that her loved one remember her. The final **sestet** adds a more realistic and compassionate hope that a trace of her will always be with him but that he should not allow her death to be a burden he carries forever. The regularity of the form suggests the containment of her feelings in a difficult situation. A similarly rigid structure is seen in 'Do not go gentle' although this poem takes the form of a **villanelle**, a nineteen-line poem that follows a **regular rhyme scheme**. This strict form, combined with the ten-syllable **rhythm** and regular three-line **stanzas**, suggests that Thomas, like Rossetti, is using this rigid pattern to perhaps contain his grief at the prospect of his father's approaching death. The last **stanza** is a direct address to his father, in which he seems to suggest a desperate need to keep his father with him on any terms.

It is clear that both poets see death as a permanent loss but the poets have different views about how one should approach it. In 'Remember' death is metaphorically described as a journey into a distant and **'silent land'**. The speaker will be voiceless in death and therefore has no power to keep their relationship alive. The use of **anadiplosis** – '**I am gone away/ Gone far away ..**' emphasises the permanency of death and the breaking of the connection between them. However, she is accepting of her fate and just wants her loved one to remember her once she has gone. This is very different to Thomas' poem where death is seen as something that should be fought against. It is portrayed as a painful, emotional event as he states '**old age should burn**' and that elderly people should '**rage, rage against the dying of the light**'. The **words** '**burn**' and '**rage**' suggest a searing pain and a fury, perhaps the pain of the dying man who realises that life and all its opportunities are almost over. Life is linked with '**light**' and its associations with hope and optimism, whereas death is seen as '**the close of day**', with darkness and finality. Both poets, therefore, recognise the absoluteness of life's end, but they differ in their acceptance of its inevitability.

Both poets explore how death brings regret and a sense of loss. Life's experiences are over and there is no turning back. No second chances. For Rossetti, she mourns that there will be no more physical contact between the lovers to keep their relationship alive. It is only the memory which must survive: '**you can no more hold me by the hand … stay**'. The *alliterative* '**h**' sounds in '**hold me by the hand**' form an aural connection between the lovers as well as alluding to a physical one in their lives, but the speaker reminds us that death is a permanent state and that there is no returning. The *verb* '**stay**' reflects a return to a previous *rhyme* '*away*', which echoes the meaning of the line as the speaker talks about the ability she has had in life to walk away then return. The memory of her will be the only way in which she will be able to return after death. The tone is regretful and mournful in a similar way to 'Do not go gentle' although Thomas includes examples of those who fight death as they have regrets about their lives: '**Wild men who caught and sang the sun in flight**' now '**grieved it on its way**'. This *stanza* comments on '**wild men**' who seem to be daring, adventurous men who lived life to the full. They are possibly men who have lived their lives indulging in pleasure: living to excess, drinking and partying. The *metaphor* relates to these pleasure-seekers who harnessed the power of the sun but now realise it is leaving the sky and regret their hedonistic pursuits. They have no chance to properly appreciate life's opportunities so, according to the speaker, should rage against its ending. Despite both poets focusing on a sense of regret, for Rossetti it is the loss of a future, whilst for Thomas the regret is based in the past.

'Remember' and 'Do not go gentle' show us that death and mourning are very personal. Both poets give specific advice on how to react to death but from different perspectives. The final lines of Rossetti's poem encapsulate the speaker's message: that it is better if her loved one is happy in his future life rather than full of grief and despair. *Parallelism* is used to emphasise the different situations left for the speaker's loved one. The *repetitive structure* and use of *antithesis* reinforces the differences between the two scenarios. He must '**forget**' and '**smile**' rather than '**remember**' and be '**sad**'. Employing the *second-person* and the *modal verb* '**should**' reflect the forceful voice of the speaker as she expresses the desire for him to be happy. For Thomas, the shift in the pattern of the lines to ABAA, as the *villanelle* comes to an end, echoes a shift from the general to the very personal as Thomas now addresses '**my father**' directly using the *personal pronoun* '**you**'. There is an emotional conflict which is established with the *oppositional verbs* in the line '**Curse, bless, me now**'; the speaker seems desperate to keep his father with him on any terms. At the end, the *refrain* '**Do not go gentle into that good night,/ Rage, rage against the dying of the light**' is *repeated* for the final time. The relentless *repetition* perhaps shows the inevitability of death and how it cannot be avoided: that we all have to accept in the end our own mortality. Much like Rossetti's '**silent land**' death is seen as a place of silence and darkness after the light of life has been extinguished. Despite their very different journeys when facing death, both poets end on a note of acceptance and resignation.

Compare the ways the writers present the world in 'If – ' and 'Prayer Before Birth'.

If –		**Prayer Before Birth**
The world is difficult but manageable if we tackle it in the right way.	In both 'If –' and 'Prayer Before Birth', the poets present the readers with worlds that are difficult to navigate, but the messages are very different.	The world is difficult and the persona is searching desperately for a way to manage it
The world is dangerous and chaotic. **'If you can keep your head when all about you/ Are losing theirs and blaming it on you'.** The *conditional* offers the reader different scenarios, challenging us to consider how we would react in them. The speaker advises us to keep calm.	In both poems, the world is dangerous.	The world is dangerous. The speaker is full of childish fears such as **'bloodsucking bat or the rat or the stoat or the club-footed ghoul'**. The *polysyndetic list* shows the rising terror of the child. The structure of the poem follows that of a prayer with the *repeated* structure of every stanza beginning with **'I am not yet born'** and concluding with **'me'**. This *epistrophe* helps create the strong sense of the foetus and its huge worries and concerns about entering the world with its array of dangers.
The world is full of deceit shown in **'if you can ….being lied about/ don't deal in lies'**. Yet the speaker tells us to stay honest. There is a strong *imperative* to reject the mendacity of the world, a clear instruction to stay honest. The energy of the *regular rhythm* captures a sense of determined enthusiasm.	In both poems, there is a presentation of the world as a place full of trickery and deceit.	The world is full of deceit as **'the human race….with wise lies lure me'**. The persona is already aware of the slick lies and insincerity of the human race. The *alliteration* captures how slick and skilful those who deceive are, and how hard it is to resist this deceit.

56 | Exam Success

The world is tough but fulfilling as **'if you can fill the unforgiving minute/ With sixty seconds' worth of distance run'**. The poet puts his faith in people. The relentless passing of time is captured in the *metaphor* of the minute being **'unforgiving'**, acknowledging that the world will not stand still or be controlled by us, but then the next line changes it to **'sixty seconds'** worth of **'distance run'**, suggesting that life must be lived to the maximum, that if we put effort into our lives then we will be fulfilled and our time in the world will be positive.

Yet both poets see some good in the world.

The comfort of nature makes the world a better place.

'water to dandle me, grass to grow for me, trees to talk/ to me, sky to sing to me, birds and a white light/ in the back of my mind to guide me'. There is a feeling of hope and anticipation created through the *alliteration* and *lyrical rhythm*. There is a sense that the foetus will enjoy a harmony with nature that will allow its individuality to flourish and to retain a sense of morality. The *metaphor* of the **'white light'**, symbol of bright hope and clarity, as a guiding force gives us hope that the persona will use nature to resist the evil of the world.

There is an optimistic ending as the poem reaches its conclusion.

'Yours is the Earth and everything that's in it/ And- which is more- you'll be a Man, my son!' The strong *declarative sentence* shows how following the advice will lead to being successful in the world. Kipling was writing to his son, giving him a personal instruction manual to deal with life but the poem's advice resonates with us all. The final *exclamatory statement* captures the writer's excitement that his child is becoming a man with all that this embodies.

Both poets shift the patterns of their poems at the end, but with very different messages about the world.

There is a pessimistic ending as the poem reaches its conclusion. **'Let them not make me a stone and let them not spill me./ Otherwise kill me.'**

Unlike the previous *stanzas*, this *stanza* is only two lines and loses the **'I am not yet born: O…'** This perhaps shows the speaker's vulnerability, that it has stopped asking for help as it knows there is no help coming. The persona does not want to be a **'stone'**- something with no emotions or to lose its identity through being **'spill'**(ed). The persona wants to die before being born if it means life will lead to it becoming emotionless or without personality.

Revision Guide for IGCSE Edexcel Poetry Anthology

Compare the ways the writers present the world in 'If –' and 'Prayer Before Birth'.

In both 'If –' and 'Prayer Before Birth', the poets present the readers with worlds that are difficult to navigate, but the messages are very different. The poem 'If –' is a poem written by a father to his young son, advising him on how to live life in a moral, responsible way that will bring his son happiness and success in a tricky world whereas in 'Prayer Before Birth', MacNeice assumes the persona of a foetus who is praying for safety and help in the terrifying and dangerous world they are about to enter but finding little comfort as they receive no answer from a silent, unresponsive god.

Both poets present a world that is dangerous. 'If –' opens with the **conditional 'If'**, and continues to use it as a *refrain*. The **conditional** offers the reader different scenarios, challenging us to consider how we would react in them. The opening situation, **'If you can keep your head when all about you/ Are losing theirs and blaming it on you'** suggests that the world is a turbulent, stressful place where people **'lose'** their heads and blame others. The need to be calm and logical in dangerous, volatile situations that the world will throw at us, is created from the opening. Similarly, in 'Prayer Before Birth', the world is presented as threatening through the persona of an unborn child who states, **'I am not yet born'**. There is a voice of a small child who fears the **'bloodsucking bat or the rat or the stoat or the/ club-footed ghoul'**. The *polysyndetic list* creates a childish tone to the persona's rising fears, as it adds to its fantasy list of nighttime terrors, almost with a nursery rhyme feel. This creates empathy for the little baby and its innocent fears of the horrors that exist. The persona prays for safety, asking the god to whom it prays to **'hear me'**. The form of the poem follows that of a prayer with the *repeated* structure of every stanza beginning with **'I am not yet born'** and concluding with **'me'**. This *epistrophe* helps create the strong sense of the foetus and its huge worries and concerns about entering the world with its array of dangers.

In both poems, there is a presentation of the world as a place full of trickery. In 'If –', the writer exhorts his son to **'if you can ... being lied about/ don't deal in lies'**. There is a strong *imperative* to reject the mendacity of the world, a clear instruction to stay honest. The energy of the *regular rhythm* captures a sense of determined enthusiasm, so that the reader is convinced that it is possible to stay true and strong even in a deceitful world. Yet in 'Prayer Before Birth', the trickery is presented as hard to resist. The unborn child acknowledges that the **'human race ... with wise lies lure me'** and is already aware of the slick lies and insincerity of the human race. The *alliteration* captures how slick and skilful those who deceive are, showing how easy it will be for the baby to be tricked. Unlike 'If' there is a helplessness, almost an acceptance about how deceit and lies will prevail.

Yet both poets see some good in the world. In 'Prayer Before Birth', the only positive in the world seems to come through nature. The persona prays for **'water to dandle me, grass to grow for me, trees to talk/ to me, sky to sing to me, birds and a white light/ in the back of my mind to guide me'**, asking for a connection with nature. There is a feeling of hope and anticipation created through the *alliteration* and *lyrical rhythm*. There is a sense that the foetus will enjoy a harmony with nature that will allow its individuality to flourish and to retain a sense of morality. The *metaphor* of the **'white light'**, symbol of bright hope and clarity, as a guiding force gives us hope that the persona will use nature to resist the evil of the world and keep its inherent goodness intact. However, in 'If –', the persona places hope in people, not nature, saying that **'if you can fill the unforgiving minute/ With sixty seconds' worth of distance run'**. The relentless passing of time is captured in the *metaphor* of the minute being **'unforgiving'**, acknowledging that the world will not stand still or be controlled by us, but then the next line changes it to **'sixty seconds'** worth of **'distance run'**, suggesting that life must be lived to the maximum, that if we put effort into our lives then we will be fulfilled and our time in the world will be positive.

Both poets shift the patterns of their poems at the end, but with very different messages about the world. In 'If –', the final *stanza* changes the pattern as Kipling moves to his conclusion: that if we follow his advice, then **'Yours is the Earth and everything that's in it/ And- which is more- you'll be a Man, my son!'** The strong *declarative sentence* shows how following the advice will lead to being successful in the world. Kipling was writing to his son, giving him a personal instruction manual to deal with life but the poem's advice resonates with us all. The final *exclamatory statement* captures the writer's excitement that his child is becoming a man with all that this embodies. In 'Prayer Before Birth', MacNeice also shifts the pattern with **'Let them not make me a stone and let them not spill me./ Otherwise kill me.'** Unlike the previous *stanzas*, this *stanza* is only two lines and loses the **'I am not yet born: O…'** This perhaps shows the speaker's vulnerability, that it has stopped asking for help as it knows there is no help coming. The persona does not want to be a **'stone'**- something with no emotions or to lose its identity through being **'spill'**(ed). The persona wants to die before being born if it means life will lead to it becoming emotionless or without personality. MacNeice ends his poem on a bleak note asking us to consider the harsh world that helpless unborn children are entering, while Kipling ends his poem encouraging his son to engage with the world and become master of it.

Compare how the writers present strong feelings in 'Search For My Tongue' and 'Half-caste'.

Search For My Tongue		Half-caste
Even the title shows the importance of finding one's roots as the word **'Search'** captures how she is actively looking for her identity, her mother tongue - she feels strongly about this.	**Both poets feel strongly about their identity.**	The title **'Half-caste'** shows how the speaker knows that he is defined by his colour. He is acknowledging how society gives him a label that is linked to his racial background and feels strongly about the label.
Free verse with no formal rhyme or rhythm creates the sense of a conversation. The poem *opens* with a sense of an on-going conversation with **'You ask me'** and **'I ask you'**. The *tone* is confrontational and perhaps one of frustration, as she challenges us to imagine what it must be like to struggle with expressing ourselves.	**Both poems open by engaging the reader, forcing us to listen to the ideas and perhaps question our own prejudices and assumptions as the speakers show their frustrations.**	The poem opens with a meek, humble request for the reader, or the person being addressed, to **'Excuse me'**. There is humour as he highlights the nonsense of the term **'half-caste'**, which implies that a mixed-race person is lesser in some way - so much so that they have to stand on **'one leg'**.
		The humorous *tone* of the humble opening *stanza* abruptly changes to a confrontational *tone* as the speaker demands that society needs to **'explain yuself'**.
		The phrase is *repeated*, putting continuous pressure on the reader to explain why we use the racist definition of people of mixed-race.
The poet calls the language of the country she lives in a **'foreign tongue'**. The *phrase* suggests the alien and unknown, adding onto the feelings that she doesn't belong and indeed has a fragmented identity.	**Both poets feel alienation.**	**'I half-caste human being/ cast half-a-shadow'**
		Agard feels as if he is separated from mainstream society by being labelled **'half-caste'**. The line suggests that he believes that people see him as not fully human, that he is not really seen or important in society. This idea of a half-shadow links to Gothic ideas of the supernatural, reflecting how society often fears anyone who is different.

Bhatt feels anger and disgust at her lost language with '**rot,/ rot and die in your mouth**' The *repetition* of '**rot**' is a revolting image and the way the *verb* '**rot**' ends one line and then is immediately repeated at the start of the next powerfully captures the extent of her disgust and the feeling of loss she has. The *consonantal* sounds '**rot**' and '**spit**' capture her frustration. The *monosyllabic words* are stilted; she uses simple language, reflecting her lack of connection with the language she has to use in order to communicate.	**Both poets feel anger.**	Anger in the expletive '**ah rass**' captures his disgust at the racism. This phrase forms one distinct line, suggesting how his anger spills out mid-way through his argument. The poem is in *free verse* with short lines and limited punctuation which creates a fast-paced poem that hammers home his message: that prejudice is wrong. The use of *phonetic spelling* and the Caribbean dialect called *Creole* work together to highlight how Agard takes control of his identity through his language.
મને હતું કે આખૂખી ભ આખૂખી ભાષા Yet in the middle, the structure changes suddenly and dramatically with the *stanza* in Gujarati. By placing the Gujarati in the middle, she shows its central importance to her as a person. There is a sense of pride in the beautiful script. The Gujarati script also forces the reader to understand her feeling of alienation. Bhatt is educating us, ensuring that we understand the lives of immigrants who do not have English as a first language.	**Both poets feel pride in their heritage.**	Agard uses *imagery* - '**yu mean when picasso** **mix red an green** **is a half-caste canvas**' to present his message that his mixed identity is beautiful, to allow us to understand how we see art, which blends colours to create something beautiful and of high-value. We should extend this to race, with the message that mixed-race people should also be valued. He is proud of his heritage, and this is further emphasised by the lack of a capital letter for '**picasso**'. This, and the disregard throughout the poem of traditional rules of punctuation and capitalisation, captures his pride in his own language and identity.
The poem *ends* on a note of hope as she rediscovers her mother tongue as it '**grows…grows…it blossoms.**' The *repetition* of '**grows**' creates a powerful sense of energy, enhanced by the unfolding *clauses* which build a sense of development, and the poem ends with a sense of celebration that she has regained her language and her identity. She uses an extended *metaphor* of a flourishing plant that '**blossoms**' and so captures ideas of hope and rejuvenation.	**Both poems end with a feeling of hope**	At the very end, Agard promises that he will share his experiences and culture with us as. '**I will tell yu** **de other half** **of my story**' There is a sense of hope that, with the end of pointless labels and discrimination, we can have a fuller, richer society.

Compare how the writers present strong feelings in 'Search For My Tongue' and 'Half-caste'.

Both Agard in 'Half-caste' and Bhatt in 'Search For My Tongue' use their poems to convey an array of strong feelings. 'Half-caste' is a powerful poem that reflects the poet's anger as he challenges stereotypes and discrimination through the speaker's exploration of the word 'half-caste'. This is a derogatory word for people of mixed-race, and throughout the poem, the speaker ridicules it so that the reader is encouraged to confront their prejudices. Similarly, in 'Search For My Tongue', Bhatt explores ideas of identity as the persona tells us her fears of forgetting her original language, her mother tongue, as she lives in a foreign country.

Both poets feel strongly about their identity and this is reflected in the titles. The title 'Search For My Tongue' shows the importance of finding one's roots as the *word* '**Search**' captures how she is actively looking for her identity, her mother tongue, while Agard's title '**Half-caste**' shows how the speaker knows that he is defined by his colour. He is acknowledging how society gives him a label that is linked to his racial background and expressing how strongly he feels about this label.

Both poems open with engagement with the reader, forcing us to listen to their ideas and perhaps question our own prejudices and assumptions as the writers show their frustrations. 'Search For My Tongue' uses *free verse* with no formal rhyme or rhythm and this creates the sense of a conversation. The poem *opens* with a sense of this on-going conversation with '**You ask me**' and '**I ask you**'. The *tone* is confrontational and perhaps one of irritation as Bhatt challenges us to imagine what it must be like to struggle with expressing ourselves. In the same way, 'Half-caste' immediately engages with the reader, although it opens with a meek, humble request for the reader, or the person being addressed, to '**excuse me**'. There is humour as he highlights the nonsense of the term '**half-caste**', which implies a mixed-race person is lesser in some way- so much so that they have to stand on '**one leg**'. The humorous *tone* of the humble opening *stanza* abruptly changes to a confrontational *tone,* similar to 'Search For My Tongue', as the speaker demands that society needs to '**explain yuself**'. The phrase is *repeated*, putting continuous pressure on the reader to explain why we use the racist definition of people of mixed-race, and making his strong feelings about the need to challenge discrimination very clear.

There is a complex mix of emotions in both poems. A feeling of alienation is evident in 'Search For My Tongue' with the persona calling the language of the country she lives in a '**foreign tongue**'. The *phrase* suggests the alien and unknown, creating the feeling that she doesn't belong and indeed has a fragmented identity, while in 'Half-caste' the line '**I half-caste human being cast half-a-shadow**' highlights how Agard feels as if he is separated from mainstream society by being labelled '**half-caste**'. The line suggests that he believes that people see him as not fully human, that he is not really seen or important in society. This idea of a half-shadow links to Gothic ideas of the supernatural, reflecting how society often fears anyone who is different. Yet this is not the only emotion. Bhatt reveals her anger and disgust at her lost language in the line '**rot,/ rot and die in your mouth**'.

The way the ***verb* 'rot'** ends one line and then is immediately ***repeated*** at the start of the next, powerfully captures the extent of her disgust and the feeling of loss she has and the ***consonantal*** sounds **'rot'** and **'spit'** capture her frustration. The ***monosyllabic*** words are stilted; she uses simple language, reflecting her lack of connection and uncertainty with the language she has to use in order to communicate. There is anger as well in 'Half-caste' with the ***expletive* 'ah rass'**, which captures his disgust at the racism. This phrase forms one distinct line, suggesting how his anger spills out mid-way through his argument. The poem is in ***free verse*** with short lines and limited punctuation, which creates a fast-paced poem that hammers home his message: that prejudice is wrong.

Yet there are positive emotions as well in both poems. In **'Search For My Tongue'**, the ***structure*** changes suddenly and dramatically with the ***stanza*** in Gujarati મને હતું કે આખૂખી ભ આખૂખી ભાષા. By placing the Gujarati in the middle, she shows its central importance to her as a person, and there is a sense of pride in the beautiful script. The Gujarati script also forces the reader to understand her feeling of alienation. Bhatt is educating us, ensuring that we understand the lives of immigrants who do not have English as a first language. In the same way, Agard expresses pride through the use of ***phonetic spelling*** and the Caribbean dialect called ***Creole***, which work together to highlight how Agard takes control of his identity through his language. Furthermore, he uses ***imagery*** of **'yu mean when picasso mix red an green is a half-caste canvas'** to present his message that his mixed identity is beautiful, to allow us to understand how we see art, which blends colours to create something beautiful and of high-value. We should extend this to race, with the message that mixed-race people should also be valued. Like Bhatt, he is proud of his heritage, and this is further emphasised by the lack of a capital letter for **'picasso'**. This, and the disregard throughout the poem of traditional rules of punctuation and capitalisation, captures his delight in his own language and identity.

The final ***stanzas*** of both poems ***end*** on a note of hope. Bhatt rediscovers her mother tongue as it **'grows… grows…it blossoms'**. The ***repetition*** of **'grows'** creates a powerful sense of energy, enhanced by the unfolding ***clauses*** which build a sense of development, and the poem ends with a sense of celebration that she has regained her language and her identity. She uses an extended ***metaphor*** of a flourishing plant that **'blossoms'** and so captures feelings of hope and rejuvenation. Similarly, in Half-caste, at the very end, Agard promises that he will share his experiences and culture with us when he **'will tell yu/ de other half/ of my story'**. There is a sense of hope that, with the end of pointless labels and discrimination, we can have a fuller, richer society, just as the message at the end of 'Search For My Tongue' offers the promise of a world where everyone's heritage is valued.

Compare how the writers present difficult situations in 'Blessing' and 'War Photographer'.

War Photographer		Blessing
The poem explores the difficulties of a profession which mean that the photographer has to record dreadful sights and experiences without being able to help, and the isolation the persona experiences as a result of his job. It focuses on one individual's harrowing experiences.	**Both poets present difficult situations and the resilience of the people who deal with these situations.**	Dharker focuses on a community in India's constant struggle to survive and access water, using one incident to capture the joy a burst water pipe can bring to the suffering people.
The poem opens in the '**dark room**' of '**rural England**' with a sense of peace and isolation after the chaotic horror of war zones such as '**Belfast. Beirut.**' '**Priest**' and '**mass**' : the *religious imagery* connects the photographer to the idea of a vocational calling. It is the photographer's duty to share his images with the public in order to try to stop the suffering- almost a sacred duty. By using *religious imagery*, Duffy is exploring the photographer's job and his emotions surrounding it. It could be that the photographer feels overwhelming guilt for recording the suffering rather than stopping it and is seeking atonement (forgiveness) for this sin. Or perhaps the *religious imagery* shows the utmost respect with which the photographer handles the images of suffering.	**Both poems take the reader to very different places.**	Dharker transports us to the vicious heat of India with the simile '**The skin cracks like a pod**' capturing the human skin cracking in the brutal heat; the *consonantal* '**k**' sounds mimic the pain of this. '**Pod**' implies regeneration and growth but here, without moisture, we are reminded of how fragile life is. '**There never is enough water.**' The second line is bare and matter-of-fact in *tone*. '**Never**' reminds us how this challenging situation is permanent.

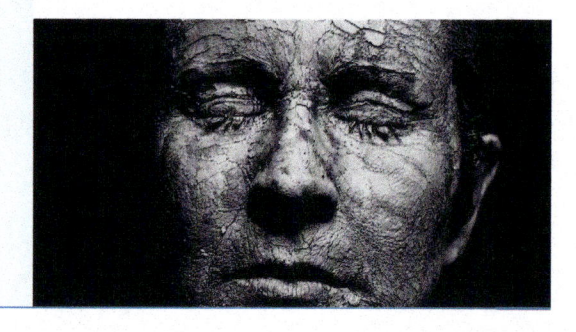

64 | Exam Success

'**Solutions slop in trays**'- the *sibilance* illustrates the unsteady process of developing these photos. The photographer needed to be detached and professional while taking the photographs but now, in the safety of the dark room, his emotion in response to the horror is evident in his unsteady hands. Or perhaps it suggests the inadequacy of politics in that '**solutions**' to the world's troublespots are messy and ineffective. There is a **tone** of contempt in the use of the *verb* '**slop**': Duffy could be expressing her anger at world leaders' attempts to stop the suffering of ordinary people.	**Both poets express anger at how governments fail to resolve difficult situations.**	Dharker asks us to '**Imagine the drip**' (of water). She is challenging us, complacently living with the luxury of running water, to put ourselves into the lives of India's poor where the drip of water is something special. '**voice of a kindly god**' Perhaps there is an ironic tone here- the gods do not protect the people who die daily through lack of fresh water.
There is a sense of drama which marks a change in this *stanza* with the *phrase* '**something is happening**'. The reader watches the photograph developing with the photographer, which creates a sense of immediacy and involvement, especially as it's in the *present tense*. The photograph is developing- a picture of a body that starts to '**twist**'- this is a painful *verb*, suggesting a body writhing in pain, perhaps someone tortured or dying.	**Both poets create a sense of drama mid-way through the poems.**	The water pipe '**bursts, silver crashes to the ground and the flow has found a roar of tongues**'. The dynamic *verbs* '**bursts**' and '**crashes**' work with the *enjambment* to create a sense of energetic movement as the water pumps out. The *aural nature* of these verbs and also '**roar**' captures the sounds of the scene and the excitement as the people call out at the unexpected, welcome event.
The readers of the newspapers have eyes that '**prick with tears**', which shows the shallowness of those reading the papers. '**prick**' suggests a tiny amount of response from the reader and shows the lack of involvement from the average Sunday paper reader- how little they are affected by what they see and read. Again, it challenges us and our own response to the evil taking place in the world and how we ignore it.	**There are different reactions to the situations.**	The people are '**screaming in the liquid sun**'. The sound is one of pure joy and appreciation, enhanced by the *image* of light, symbol of warmth and hope.
The poem ends with the photographer coming full circle. He is flying out to another troublespot to take more photographs which will be developed and published, and nothing will change. The *cyclical nature* of the poem illustrates how suffering will continue and shows a pessimistic view of human nature and its inability to avoid conflict.	**The endings of the poems both highlight the ongoing nature of the difficult situations.**	The poem ends with the lines '**blessing sings/ over their small bones**' The *verb* '**sings**' suggests the voice of the god can now be heard as the children of the slum benefit from the burst water pipe. Yet the final *noun phrase* '**small bones**' reminds us of how frail and vulnerable the children are and that the scarcity of water will return. The water pipe bursting is only a temporary respite.

Compare how the writers present difficult situations in 'Blessing' and 'War Photographer'.

Both Duffy in 'War Photographer' and Dharker in 'Blessing' present difficult situations and the resilience of the people who deal with these situations. In 'War Photographer', the poem explores the difficulties of a profession which means that the photographer has to record dreadful sights and experiences without being able to help, and the isolation the persona experiences as a result of his job. It focuses on one individual's harrowing experience, whereas in 'Blessing', Dharker focuses on a community in India's constant struggle to survive and access fresh water. She describes the joy a burst water pipe brings to the suffering people, and how it eases a difficult situation, albeit momentarily.

Both poems take the reader to very different places. 'War Photographer' opens in the **'dark room'** of **'rural England'** where there is a sense of peace and isolation after the chaotic horror of war zones such as **'Belfast. Beirut'**. The photographer is described as a **'priest'** taking **'mass'** as he develops his photographs, and the *religious imagery* connects the photographer to the idea of a vocational calling. It is the photographer's duty to share his images with the public in order to try to stop the suffering- almost a sacred duty. By using *religious imagery,* Duffy is exploring the photographer's job and his emotions surrounding it. It could be that the photographer feels overwhelming guilt for recording the suffering rather than stopping it and is seeking atonement for this sin. Clearly, the process of developing the photos helps the photographer process his difficult experiences. Whereas in 'Blessing', Dharker transports us to the vicious heat of India where **'the skin cracks like a pod.'** The *simile* captures the human skin cracking in the brutal heat; the *consonantal* **'k'** sounds mimic the pain of this. **'Pod'** implies regeneration and growth but here, without moisture, we are reminded of how fragile life is. The second line is bare and matter-of-fact in *tone* as **'there never is enough water'**, the word **'never'** reminding us how this challenging situation is permanent.

Both poets express anger at how governments fail to resolve difficult situations. In 'War Photographer', **'solutions slop in trays'** with the *sibilance* illustrating the unsteady process of developing these photos. The photographer needed to be detached and professional while taking the photographs but now, in the safety of the dark room, his emotion in response to the horror is evident in his unsteady hands. Yet perhaps it suggests the inadequacy of politics in that **'solutions'** to the world's troublespots are messy and ineffective. There is a *tone* of contempt in the use of the *verb* **'slop'** as Duffy could be expressing her anger at world leaders' attempts to stop the suffering of ordinary people. Similarly, Dharker expresses anger at a situation where leaders fail to provide basic needs, as she asks us to **'Imagine the drip'** (of water). She is challenging us, complacently living with the luxury of running water, to put ourselves into the lives of India's poor where the drip of water is something special. She also states that the sound of the drip is the **'voice of a kindly god'**. Perhaps there is an ironic *tone* here: the gods do not protect the people who die daily through lack of fresh water, and here she perhaps criticises both organised religion and governments who ignore the difficult situations that the ordinary people encounter.

Both poets create a sense of drama mid-way through the poems. In 'War Photographer', we are told that **'something is happening'** and the reader watches the photograph developing with the photographer, which creates a sense of immediacy and involvement, especially as it's in the *present tense*. A photograph is developing: a picture of a body that **'twist'**(s). This is a painful *verb*, suggesting a body writhing in pain, perhaps someone being tortured or dying, experiencing the most difficult of situations. However, in 'Blessing' the drama is something wonderful as **'the municipal pipe bursts,/ silver crashes to the ground/ and the flow has found/ a roar of tongues.'** The *dynamic verbs* **'bursts'** and **'crashes'** work with the *enjambment* to create a sense of energetic movement as the water pumps out, relieving the challenging situation of a lack of water. The *aural* nature of these *verbs* and also the *noun* **'roar'** capture the sounds of the scene and the excitement as the people call out at the unexpected, welcome event.

There are different reactions to the situations. In 'War Photographer', the readers of the newspapers have eyes that **'prick with tears'**, highlighting the shallowness of those reading the papers. The *verb* **'prick'** suggests a tiny amount of response from the reader and shows the lack of involvement from the average Sunday paper reader- how little they are affected by the terrible situations that they see and read about. Duffy challenges us and our own response to the evil taking place in the world and how we ignore it. However, in 'Blessing', Dharker shows the huge emotion of those involved who are **'screaming in the liquid sun'**, the sound of pure joy and appreciation enhanced by the *image* of light, a symbol of warmth and hope.

The endings of the poems both highlight the ongoing nature of the difficult situations. 'War Photographer' ends with the photographer coming full circle, flying out to another trouble spot to take more photographs, which will be developed and published and nothing will change. The *cyclical nature* of the poem illustrates how suffering will continue and shows a pessimistic view of human nature and its inability to avoid conflict. Conversely, Dharker's poem ends on a note of temporary hope as the **'blessing sings/ over their small bones'**. The *verb* **'sings'** suggests the voice of the god can now be heard as the children of the slum benefit from the burst water pipe. Yet the final *noun phrase* **'small bones'** reminds us of how frail and vulnerable the children are, and that the scarcity of water will return. The water pipe bursting is only a temporary respite from the relentless water poverty that the poem describes. At the end of each poem, there is an uneasy sense that it will be very difficult to permanently resolve the difficult situations in which the people exist.

Compare how the writers present ideas of power in 'The Tyger' and 'La Belle Dame sans Merci'.

The Tyger

Blake uses the fictional creation of a beautiful but deadly tiger in a divine blacksmith's forge to question how and why an all-powerful God deliberately introduces danger and evil into the world.

Both poets explore ideas of power: who holds power and to what ends it is used.

La Belle Dame sans Merci

The *ballad* tells the story of a knight who falls in love with a beautiful cruel woman who uses her power to bewitch him and leave him broken and miserable.

The tiger's power is established by referring to it as **'burning bright'**. The *plosive alliteration* of the **'b'** sounds ensure an energetic, explosive start while the *word* **'burning'** suggests the deadly nature of the tiger, as fire can easily become uncontrollable and destructive. Yet the tiger's power also lies in its beauty as it is also **'bright'**, suggesting that it is glowing and aesthetically lovely. Blake sets up one of his many unanswered questions here as he wonders how something stunning can also be so terrible.

Both poets present the reader with a central figure that explores the idea of power.

The poem opens with a speaker asking a question of a knight who is **'alone and palely loitering'**. The knight is immediately established as isolated and abandoned with the *phrase* **'palely loitering'** suggesting that he has lost his natural healthy colour, and is perhaps ill. There is a lack of purpose in the *verb* **'loitering'** which reveals how he has been stripped of motivation and action.

The poet imagines the tiger being created in a divine blacksmith's forge with **'anvil'** and **'furnace'**. Blake depicts God as a strong blacksmith who has the power to **'twist the sinews'** of the tiger's heart into place. Blake makes it clear that the existence of the tiger is no accident: it was a deliberate act of creation. The flurry of *questions* that structure the poem becomes ever more insistent, as the poet's desire for answers becomes stronger, asking **'What the hammer? what the chain…?'**

Both poems explore the power of the mystical or the unexplained.

Keats allows the knight to take over the narrative and tell his story of how he met a woman who is **'full beautiful - a faery's child,/…And her eyes were wild'**. The woman is positioned as desirable with the *intensifier* **'full'** adding to the *adjective* **'beautiful'** to create an impression of a stunning woman. Certainly, in the male speaker's view, she is defined first by her physical attraction which in itself is powerful. Yet it is her otherness which gives her real power. She is unusual as she is a **'faery's child'** and while this perhaps adds to her attraction in the eyes of the knight, it also establishes her as possibly dangerous, operating under different rules to conventional society.

The poet questions God's intentions. He asks if God was happy with his creation, whether he **'smile'** (d) at his finished product, and then asks **'Did he who made the Lamb make thee?'** This question ponders how the same God who made the vulnerable, gentle lamb can also have made the dangerous tiger who will want to destroy it.

In both poems, there is an uneasy sense that power can be dangerous.

The poem also ends with a sense of weak vulnerability. The knight dreams of the other men who have been bewitched by the belle dame, **'pale kings, and princes too,/ Pale warriors, death-pale …They cried - 'La Belle Dame sans Merci/ Thee hath in thrall!''** The *repetition* of **'pale'** reminds us of the knight's description at the start. All these powerful men of wealth and status are drained of their vitality- no one is safe from the woman's spells and charms. The voices of the men who **'cried'** adds to the sense of drama as we hear their urgent calls of warning. The poem then concludes with the knight echoing the original speaker's words that **'no birds sing'**.

Revision Guide for IGCSE Edexcel Poetry Anthology | 69

Compare how the poets present ideas of power in 'The Tyger' and 'La Belle Dame sans Merci'.

The poets of both 'The Tyger' and 'La Belle Dame sans Merci' explore ideas of power: who holds power and to what ends it is used. In 'The Tyger', Blake uses the fictional creation of a beautiful but deadly tiger in a divine blacksmith's forge to question how and why an all-powerful God deliberately introduces danger and evil into the world. Similarly, in 'La Belle Dame sans Merci' the *ballad* tells the story of a knight who falls in love with a beautiful, cruel woman who uses her power to bewitch him and leave him broken and miserable.

Both poets present the reader with a central figure that explores the idea of power. In 'The Tyger', the poem immediately addresses the tiger, establishing its importance and power by referring to it as **'burning bright'**. The *plosive alliteration* of the **'b'** sounds ensures an energetic, explosive start while the word **'burning'** suggests the deadly nature of the tiger as fire can easily become uncontrollable and destructive. Yet the tiger's power also lies in its beauty as it is also **'bright'**, suggesting that it is glowing and aesthetically lovely. Blake sets up one of his many unanswered questions here, as he wonders how something stunning can also be so terrible. Conversely, the central figure in 'La Belle Dame sans Merci' lacks power, and the poem opens with a speaker asking a question of a knight who is **'alone and palely loitering'**. The knight is immediately established as isolated and abandoned with the *phrase* **'palely loitering'** suggesting that he has lost his natural healthy colour, and is perhaps ill. There is a lack of purpose in the *verb* **'loitering'** which reveals how he has been stripped of motivation and action. Traditionally, Mediaeval knights are dynamic heroes in control of their own adventures and destinies yet in the poem the knight is a helpless victim, reflecting how Keats is subverting the expectations of the reader. The question is *repeated* as a *hook* as we wonder, along with the speaker, what has happened to the knight to leave him in such a weak, vulnerable state.

Both poems explore the power of the mystical or the unexplained. In 'The Tyger', the poet imagines the tiger being created in a divine blacksmith's forge with **'anvil'** and **'furnace'**. Blake depicts God as a strong blacksmith who has the power to **'twist the sinews'** of the tiger's heart into place. Blake makes it clear that the existence of the tiger is no accident: it was a deliberate act of creation. The flurry of *questions* that structure the poem becomes ever more insistent, as the poet's desire for answers becomes stronger, asking **'What the hammer? what the chain…?'** The *rhythm* used is *trochaic tetrameter* which reflects the pounding of the hammer in the forge, vividly conveying to the readers the enormous strength of God as he works on his creation. Alternatively, the insistent *rhythm* could capture the deliberate padding of a tiger's feet as it moves through its territory. Similarly, the powerful figure within 'La Belle Dame sans Merci' possesses supernatural powers. Keats allows the knight to take over the narrative and tell his story of how he met a woman who is **'full beautiful - a faery's child… and her eyes were wild'**. The woman is positioned as desirable with the *intensifier* **'full'** adding to the *adjective* **'beautiful'** to create an impression of a stunning woman. Certainly, in the male speaker's view, she is defined first by her physical attraction which in itself is powerful. Yet it is her otherness which gives her real power. She is unusual as she is a **'faery's child'** and while this perhaps adds to her attraction in the eyes of the knight, it also establishes her as possibly dangerous, operating under different rules to conventional society. This idea is added to with the description of her **'wild'** eyes, suggesting a savage side, unconstrained by civilised ways to behave. The *rhyme scheme* is consistent throughout the poem, which fits in with the genre of a *ballad*. Here, the *rhyme* links the words **'faery's child'** with **'wild'** which in turn highlights the supernatural element to the story and the savage power of the fierce belle dame who is the daughter of a magical being. Certainly, the power she wields enables her to place the knight under her spell as he relates how **'I made a garland for her head.... I set her on my pacing steed'**. The *simple sentences* capture his desire to please his new love. Interestingly, both actions emasculate the knight. He surrenders his male power by placing the woman on his horse; traditionally, a knight is placed high above others on his fast and powerful horse, yet here the woman is elevated, perhaps showing the way she has taken control. Similarly, the knight undertakes the domestic feminine task of weaving flowers to decorate the woman's head, again showing how she has undermined his masculine authority.

In both poems, there is an uneasy sense that power can be dangerous. Towards the end of 'The Tyger', the poet questions God's intentions. He asks if God was happy with his creation, whether he **'smile'** (d) at his finished product, and then asks **'did he who made the Lamb make thee?'** This question ponders how the same God who made the vulnerable gentle lamb can also have made the dangerous tiger who will want to destroy it. The poet questions how and why God chose to put predators into the world, and if, perhaps, this represents an abuse of power. The *tone* is incredulous, as if the poet is struggling to understand, and seems to begin to question God's decisions. The poem ends with an almost identical *stanza* to the start, suggesting that the constant questions are never answered. Blake is unable to answer the questions he poses- just as we are unable to make sense of a world where good and evil coexist. Within this uncertain world, we feel an uneasy sense of threat as essentially, we are weak and powerless against a powerful, seemingly uncaring God. In the same way, 'La Belle Dame sans Merci' also ends with a sense of weak vulnerability. The knight dreams of the other men who have been bewitched by the belle dame, **'pale kings and princes too/ Pale warriors, death-pale ...They cried - 'La Belle Dame sans Merci/ Thee hath in thrall!''** The *repetition* of **'pale'** reminds us of the knight's description at the start. All these powerful men of wealth and status are drained of their vitality- no one is safe from the woman's spells and charms. The voices of the men who **'cried'** add to the sense of drama as we hear their urgent calls of warning. The poem then concludes with the knight echoing the original speaker's words that **'no birds sing'**. Now the reader understands why the knight is alone and without purpose, and understands his despair. The *pathetic fallacy* of the dead winter landscape and the absence of life and sound from the birds, powerfully captures the bleak ending and the knight's hopelessness. The *cyclical structure* echoes the hopeless state that the knight is trapped within, and suggests that other men will fall victim to the beautiful faery's child. Like 'The Tyger', the poem ends with a lingering sense of mystical powers at work against which we are powerless.

Themes Chart

	Identity	Time	Parental influence	Place	Personal Experiences	People	Nature	Religion
If –	X		X			X		
Prayer Before Birth	X			X		X		X
Blessing				X		X	X	X
Search For My Tongue	X	X	X		X	X	X	
Half-past Two	X	X		X	X	X		
Piano	X	X	X	X	X	X		
Hide and Seek	X	X		X	X	X		
Sonnet 116		X			X	X		
La Belle	X	X		X		X	X	
Poem at Thirty-Nine	X	X	X		X	X		
War Photographer	X	X		X	X	X		X
The Tyger							X	X
My Last Duchess	X					X		
Half-caste	X				X	X		
Do not go gentle		X	X		X	X		X
Remember	X	X			X	X		

72 | *Exam Success*

Compare how the writers present ideas about place in 'Half-past Two' and 'Blessing'.

Poem 1	Topic Sentence	Poem 2

Compare how the writers present ideas about identity in 'Half-caste' and one other poem from the anthology.

Poem 1	Topic Sentence	Poem 2

Compare how the writers present ideas about personal experiences in 'Search For My Tongue' and 'Piano'.

Poem 1	Topic Sentence	Poem 2

Glossary

Explanation of terms

Adjective - a word that describes a noun **e.g. 'two long legs for walking'** in 'Half-past Two'

Adverb - a word that describes a verb **e.g. 'he stares impassively'** in 'War Photographer'

Alliteration - repetition of the same sounds in words that are next to or near one another e.g **'Tyger, Tyger, burning bright' in 'The Tyger'**

Anadiplosis - using the words at the end of a clause to begin the next **e.g. 'I am gone away/ Gone far away' in 'Remember'**

Anaphora - repetition of the same words or phrases at the beginning of consecutive lines **e.g. 'Into the smell … Into the silent noise .. Into the air' in 'Half-past Two'**

Antithesis - a device that places opposite ideas parallel to each other **e.g. 'dancing/ in a yoga meditation' in 'Poem at Thirty-Nine'**

Assonance - a repetition of vowel sounds in words that appear close together **e.g 'long legs for walking' in 'Half-past Two'**

Asyndetic list - a list which leaves out conjunctions **e.g. 'cooking, writing, chopping wood' in 'Poem at Thirty-Nine'**

Auditory imagery - the creation of mental imagery through the use of sounds **e.g. 'crashes… roar' in 'Blessing'**

Ballad - a type of narrative poem that tells a story usually written in four-line stanzas

Caesura - a pause in a line of poetry **e.g. 'Don't move. Don't breathe.' in 'Hide and Seek'**

Compound word - words that are connected together to form a new word with a new meaning **e.g. 'fever-dew' in La Belle Dame sans Merci**

Conditional - a subordinate clause that sets up a hypothetical situation and used with a main clause to show consequences **e.g. 'If you can keep your head …..Yours is the Earth' in 'If – '**

Creole - a language that is created from the blending of two or more languages **e.g. 'so spiteful dem dont want de sun pass/ ah rass' in 'Half-caste'**

Cyclical structure - a narrative where the story ends in a way that connects back to the beginning **e.g. 'War Photographer'**

Declarative sentence - a sentence that makes a statement **e.g. 'Yours is the Earth' in 'If –'**

Direct speech - the actual words spoken **e.g. 'Come and find me!' in 'Hide and Seek'**

Dramatic Monologue - a poem written in the form of a speech delivered by one persona **e.g 'My Last Duchess'**

Enjambment - when a line of poetry ends with no punctuation so the meaning runs onto the next line **e.g. 'Sometimes the sudden rush/ of fortune' in 'Blessing'**

Exclamatory sentence - a sentence that expresses a strong emotion or feeling **e.g. 'you'll be a Man, my son!' in 'If –'**

Extended metaphor - a metaphor that is developed over several lines **e.g. the metaphor of the game in 'Hide and Seek'**

Eulogy - a piece of writing that commemorates somebody who has died

Free verse - an open form of poetry that does not have fixed patterns of rhythm and rhyme

Iambic pentameter - a line of poetry that consists of ten syllables with the stress on every other syllable in an unstressed/stressed pattern

Iambic tetrameter - a line of poetry that consists of eight syllables with the stress on every other syllable in an unstressed/stressed pattern

Imagery - the use of language to create a picture in our minds **e.g. 'mix red an green/ is a half-caste canvas' in 'Half-caste'**

Imperative - a verb that is used for giving commands **e.g 'Don't deal in lies' in 'If –'**

Intensifier - a word that strengthens or weakens another word **e.g. 'he'd escaped for ever' in 'Half-past Two'**

Interjection - a word or phrase used to express something in a sudden or exclamatory way **e.g. 'Yes, here you are' in 'Hide and Seek'**

Irony - language that suggests the opposite of its literal meaning **e.g 'voice of a kindly god' in 'Blessing'**

List - a number of connected ideas **e.g 'dropping of the daylight … bough of cherries …white mule' in 'My Last Duchess'**

Modal verb - a type of verb used to express possibility or obligation **e.g 'He would have grown to admire the woman' in 'Poem at Thirty-Nine'**

Metaphor - a way of describing something by referring to it as something else that has a similar characteristic **e.g 'Let them not make me a stone' in 'Prayer Before Birth'**

Monosyllabic words - words that consist of only one syllable **e.g. 'rot and die in your mouth' in 'Search For My Tongue'**

Motif - a symbolic idea or image that is repeated through the text **e.g. cooking in 'Poem at Thirty-Nine'**

Noun phrase - a phrase that includes a noun and other modifying words **e.g. 'small bones' in 'Blessing'**

Onomatopoeia - a word that imitates the sound it makes **e.g. 'splash' in 'Blessing'**

Parallelism - a structural technique where the writer repeats similar grammatical structures **e.g.** 'you should forget and smile …/ you should remember and be sad' in 'Remember'

Pathetic Fallacy - a technique whereby the natural world is attributed human emotions and feelings **e.g** the winter landscape in 'La Belle Dame sans Merci'

Personification - a technique where non-human objects or elements are given human qualities **e.g** 'Time's fool' in 'Sonnet 116'

Phonetic spelling - writing words based on how they sound **e.g.** 'yuself' in 'Half-caste'

Plosive alliteration - repetition of one of the plosive consonants - b/p/d/t **e.g** 'burning bright' in 'The Tyger'

Polysyllabic word - a word that contains more than one syllable **e.g** 'suffering' in 'War Photographer'

Polysyndetic list - the use of multiple conjunctions one after another **e.g.** 'bloodsucking bat or the rat or the stoat or the/ club-footed ghoul' in 'Prayer Before Birth'

Possessive pronoun - a word that shows that something belongs to someone **e.g.** 'My Last Duchess'

Pre-modifier - a word or phrase used before another to change its meaning **e.g.** 'dark damp smell of sand' in 'Hide and Seek'

Preposition - a word that tells you where or when something is **e.g.** 'in the boom of the tingling strings' in 'Piano'

Present continuous tense - used to convey an action that is currently happening or ongoing **e.g.** 'the heart of me weeps to belong' in 'Piano'

Refrain - a word, line or group of lines in a poem that are regularly repeated **e.g.** 'Do not go gentle into that good night'

Repetition - when a word or phrase is repeated for effect **e.g.** 'pale warriors, death-pale' in 'La Belle Dame sans Merci'

Rhetorical question - a question that does not require an answer but makes a point **e.g.** 'But where are they that sought you?' in 'Hide and Seek'

Rhyming couplets - a pair of successive lines that rhyme

Rhythm - the beat or flow of a poem

Sibilance - the repetition of letters that create a hissing or hushing sound **e.g** 'Spools of suffering' in 'War Photographer'

Simile - describing a person or object as something else using 'like' or 'as' **e.g** 'The skin cracks like a pod' in 'Blessing'

Sensory language - language that appeals to the senses **e.g.** 'roots of relish sweet/ And honey wild' in 'La Belle Dame sans Merci'

Shakespearean Sonnet - a form of poetry consisting of fourteen lines divided into three quatrains and a rhyming couplet

Stanza - a grouped set of lines within a poem

Stream of consciousness - a narrative style which tries to capture the natural, unfiltered flow of a person's thoughts

Symbolism - the use of words or images to represent an object, idea or person **e.g 'Neptune … taming a sea-horse' in 'My Last Duchess'**

Synaesthesia - a technique where a writer blends senses together for effect **e.g. 'salty dark' in 'Hide and Seek'**

Tone - the mood or atmosphere created by the writer

Trochaic tetrameter - a line of poetry which consists of four feet of stressed/unstressed syllables

Verb - an action word **e.g 'I thought I spit it out' in 'Search For My Tongue'**

Villanelle - a highly structured poem consisting of five three-line stanzas and a closing four-line stanza

Volta - a turn in an argument or thought **e.g 'Yet if you should forget me for awhile' in 'Remember'**

Printed in Great Britain
by Amazon